Bestest Words

Bestest Words

Rodney G. Miller

Parula Press

Bestest Words
Copyright © Rodney G Miller 2022
All rights reserved. No portion of this book may be reproduced, distributed, or transmitted in any form by any means without the prior written permission of the publisher, except brief quotations within reviews and specified noncommercial uses permitted by copyright law. For permission requests, write to 'Attention: Permissions' at: Parula Press, 1971 Western Avenue #147, Albany, NY 12203,
United States of America

First Edition

Notice: Every effort was made to trace the holders of copyright material. If you have any information concerning copyright material in this book, please contact the publishers at the address above.
This book features materials protected under license or by the Fair Use guidelines of Section 107 of the Copyright Act. All rights reserved to the copyright owners. The publisher has no responsibility for the persistence or accuracy of URLs for any external or third-party Internet websites referred to in this book and does not guarantee that any content on such websites is, or will remain, accurate or appropriate.

Cover Image credit: *Truthiness cartoon, Stephen Colbert*
by Greg Williams & Wikimedia Foundation is licensed under CCA-SA 2.5 Generic.
https://commons.wikimedia.org/wiki/File:Truthiness_comic.jpg

PLEASE NOTE
The blog posts in this book were originally published at the author's website: communicator.rodney-miller.com and are republished here for educational, reference, or other personal use. The book supplements collected blog posts with a bibliography, list of blog post titles/dates of publication/first lines, and an index.

Cataloging-in-Publication Data
Name: Miller, Rodney G., author
Title: *Bestest Words*
Description: Albany, NY: Parula Press, [2022] Rodney G. Miller; Includes color photos, blog post titles & first lines by date, bibliography, index
Subjects: LCSH: 1. English Language – Study and Teaching 2. Communication – Media Studies 3. Propaganda 4. Politics and Government – Democracy

ISBN: 978-1-7374895-5-9 (paperback)

Library of Congress Control Number: 2022921081

For freedoms

of

thought, speech, and association

Table of Contents

Bestest Words? 1

Hope

The Sudden Change Continues 4

Light or No… 7

The Next Thing? 10

Honestly 12

Five Rings 15

Vive Le Tour de France 17

Beyond Reason 19

Making It So 21

Votes for Action 23

Humor

What's So Funny? 26

Fabulists 28

Humor-in-Law 31

Cows & Curtains 34

When Fools Rule 36

Leadership

Homage 39

Neighbors 41

Thylacine 43

Go High 47
"Aotearoa" 50
Face Up to Absurdity 52
Tales of Two 54
Angel to Grifter to…?? 56
Rip Van Who? 59
Change or Be Changed 62
Whose Challenge? 64
Catnip Curse 67

Speaking & Writing
Why Read? Why Write? 70
What We Say 73
What the Inaugural Address Means 77
Surf 80
Violent Rhetoric 84
Reach 86
Much in Verbs 89
A Few Words 92
The -ism Family 96
Style 99
We or Me? 102
To Speak Out! 105
.0001% 109

Democracy
To Strengthen Democracy 114

Speaking Out 117

Civil Civics 119

Remembrance 121

Speak Read Write Vote 123

Now Is the Time 125

Truth, Law, and Justice

Beyond Heavens 128

Trouble with Theory 130

Accountability 133

Letters of Law 136

Media

Fall in the Suburbs 140

Pundit Propaganda 144

The Back-seat Driver 148

How Anti-social Are Social Media? 150

What's Real? 152

Polls 155

Propaganda

Not Propaganda? 158

Silly Season 161

Imagine 165

It's Time for Plain Talk 168

What to Do 171

Funny That... 176

It's the PROPAGANDA, Stu*** 178

Certainty Claims	180
The Cons	185
Foreign Fake-Fun Flops	189
Time to Chill	191
Where's the Outrage?	193
From Now On	195
Thinking for a Future	197
Blog Post Titles, First Lines, & Dates	200
Bibliography	204
Acknowledgments	208
About the Author	209
INDEX	210

Bestest Words?

Words give shape to ideas and feelings. More truly, how we interpret words as readers and listeners helps to shape understanding, relationship, or action–in turn, helping to shape us. And with "truthiness" rather than truth-telling so common in public communications, how we interpret and use words matters a lot. We rely on each other's words to "differentiate fact from opinion and the proven from the plausible" (Sayers, p. 4).

With truth-telling now needed more than ever, our ongoing effort to challenge disinformation, misinformation, and trash-talk is as necessary as reasserting values important to daily life. Perhaps, it's best to keep in mind that the strongest antidote to propaganda and its impact is our own independent thought. And keeping democracy requires that we read, listen, speak, write, and vote thoughtfully. Words used wisely can engage hope, humor, and leadership to counter propaganda and strengthen democracy.

Through the initial handling of the Covid pandemic in 2020 and a remarkable election in the United States, word-salad was so amplified at times that many days felt driven by a juggernaut heading toward ambiguous destinations. Health, safety, and freedoms previously taken for granted were continuously threatened. This was the setting, in May 2020, for starting to write these personal reflections every couple of weeks or so–to help keep perspective.

A midterm election in November 2022 delivered a much-wished-for coalition of voters, for some reprieve from the ongoing threats to health, safety, and freedoms. For any of us who believes in truth, law, and justice though, this remains a challenging time in this country and elsewhere. Outrageous public talk and too little action against the harmful behaviors of some still present hazard. Word-salad still props up news reports and talk-shows.

A relatively few bright lights in the media have found ways to probe the news, continuously urging accountability. Very often it is investigative journalists who uncover the harmful actions of public figures. Probing commentaries in the media argue for the rule of law and democratic institutions, but nonetheless offer little solution to the propaganda war.

Many in the media continue to take the bait built into propaganda, to amplify its reach to more people than otherwise possible. From earlier parroting of bandwagon claims about "elites," through the endless "B-roll" of political rallies, to the latest screams for the camera, this pseudo-news will not "just disappear." An apparently endless stream of books, along with podcasts and documentaries, expose violations of truth, law, and justice, but even the best of these offer little more than diagnosis and warning–with few advocating creative or practical remedy.

Perhaps there is promise for the news media to regain credibility and audiences through the growth of "constructive journalism." This rethinking of news practice steps beyond breaking news and investigative journalism to track public action for the common good. Constructive journalism builds on the premise that to serve democracy, quality reporting must be "critical, inspirational, nuanced, and engaging" (Constructive Institute, 2022). Meanwhile, the tabloid-based, sensational negativities of outrage, trash-talk, and exaggerations are still amplified by some public figures, social media, and gatekeepers of the mass media.

My thanks go to readers of the blog throughout the world, for your interest, comments, and feedback. In the spirit of Jacques Ellul's insight that propaganda ceases where simple dialogue begins, let's keep on seeking opportunities to advance independent thought that strengthens democracy. With best wishes to all who choose the very best words to address the challenges ahead.

December 15, 2022

Hope

The Sudden Change Continues

Seattle Policemen during Spanish Flu Epidemic, December 1918
National Archives. This image is in the Public Domain {{PD-US-expired}}
https://commons.wikimedia.org/wiki/File:Spanish_flu_in_1918,_Police_officers_in_masks,_Seattle_P
olice_Department_detail,_from-_165-WW-269B-25-police-l_(cropped).jpg

In some ways akin to the personally piercing shaft of memory each of us has for when 9/11 occurred, we will all recall our own instant of realization for the seriousness of the danger that Covid-19 posed.

For us, it was my wife's return from a monthly luncheon with friends very early in March of 2020, where no one offered anyone the customary American hug in greeting.

Since then, like many others, we remained homebound.

Family Re-run

In 2019, some newspapers were running stories about the centenary of the Spanish influenza epidemic of 1918-9. No one guessed then that the world would soon fall victim to the highly infectious and deadly pandemic of Covid-19.

The 1918 Spanish Flu retrospective stories were only highlighted personally because I'd recently discovered that my grandfather had traveled from New Zealand to the west coast of the U.S.A. in early 1919, to live and work, initially in Seattle. Nana and my dad (aged four) remained in New Zealand for almost a year before joining him, presumably, awaiting confidence on the passing of the flu.

Face Masks

A starkly iconic image that I googled showed the U.S. Army 39th regiment in late 1918 marching down the main street of Seattle in surgical masks, prior to departing for France. Another photo in Seattle showed a group of policemen wearing masks.

Who could guess that most of us would soon enough be wearing protective masks, amid unimaginable loss of life and economic disaster.

Changes

To state the obvious, this one has changed the world in so many yet-to-be-seen ways, well beyond the initial health and economic impacts. Certainly, we are seeing only the beginnings of how public communication will keep evolving.

In the short run, we see other changes. For example, a former nation-wide bakery chain has moved to distributing groceries. At least in the United States, as individual enterprise drives forward new ways to earn a living in the changed world, the competition in many industries will be fierce, even as delivery modes change.

After some trial fits and starts, I believe much education at all levels might be mainly on-line, maybe for a long time. These concerns will persist, underpinning the more immediate worries about life and death in 2020.

Some *Bennies*

Among the few benefits of the isolation are the increased interactions (remotely) with friends. As one friend put it, some of us have friends "with friends, who are bored," who help ease the isolation by finding and emailing more jokes, cartoons, and satire. Many of these are very funny.

A special benefit too is to hear more often from friends who were so often on planes—now safely working from home and emailing great memes!

Much thanks to all! May public and personal communications increasingly thrive.

With warmest wishes—be safe!

May 16, 2020

Light or No…

George Orwell, c. 1940 (1903-1950)
by Cassowary Colorizations is licensed under CCA 2.0 Generic.
https://upload.wikimedia.org/wikipedia/commons/8/82/George_Orwell%2C_c._1940_%2841928180381%29.jpg

Have you ever wondered why some people convey a sense of optimism, energy, or other positive feelings when they speak? Often, it's a smile, or eye contact, or attentiveness with facial or another nonverbal cue that puts a ray of sunlight into a conversation.

Also though, it's the words we choose that help shape such feelings. Even after the passage of so many years, inspiring speakers like Martin Luther King Jr, Sir Winston Churchill, or several Kennedys, when read again, will inspire once more.

Within their words are images of light, upbeat rhythm, and invitations to a better future. It's all in the words. Or more precisely, it's what we find in the words. Beyond what words denote is the power we give to what they suggest.

When Churchill visualized the life of the world moving "forward into broad, sunlit uplands" or spoke of the "island home," which he called upon the British to defend, he rekindled treasured feelings of belonging, of place, and a life worth living. He brought to the foreground, in minds and hearts, some hope for what might be, amid the mayhem and misery of wartime realities.

This comes to mind vividly while reading and enjoying Thomas E. Ricks's intriguing dual-biography, *Churchill & Orwell, The Fight for Freedom*, alongside George Orwell's *Homage to Catalonia*.

Despite Churchill's own periodic challenges with what he called the "black dog" of depression, the positive power of his words somehow connected within neurons, delivering hope and purpose in himself and in others. Against this, the dark words of opponents looked off-putting, or plain, or sometimes even underwhelming.

Likewise, in George Orwell's writing, amid vivid descriptions of tough times and experiences in the Spanish Civil War, he projects a spirit of hope and possibility, for the ascent of human dignity from what the ramshackle human efforts in that war might be able to accomplish.

Today, it's still possible to find words of light, separated from the projected fantasies of carnage and apocalypse that appeal to those wired for conspiracy or other dark arts, like autocrats and their co-conspirators. Slogans like one seen on a t-shirt recently, "vax–over my dead body" will appeal to those wired for the dismal, dreary, and macabre; but anyone who respects facts will reflect on that cheery thought and see the ironic inference about the destiny of the myopic.

Shifting metaphors, if we are what we eat, it's reasonable to believe that we feel what we hear, see, and read. No great discoveries in neuroscience are needed to tell us that choosing the light and the bright matters, including the words around us. Through the words that we encounter and the words that we choose, we effectively "wire" our own world view.

So, here's a short-list of words in Orwell and Churchill that leapt from just the first pages of each, as they dealt with somber scenes: Orwell, *powerful, liking, affection, spirit, bridging the gulf, liked, stuck vividly, memory, special atmosphere;* and, Churchill, *repair, heroic, best troops, best trained, fought well, think of the future, safely back, very large and powerful.*

Often, both narrated hard realities, yet their language was peppered with optimism. We should all feel free to use such words, to encourage others to use them, to add to a list to keep handy for frequent use; perhaps sometimes they can help build spirits, to navigate better paths whenever dark forces are in play. These are words that wear well and have no use-by-date.

Of course, much more is at work in Orwell's and Churchill's language than just the presence of such words. They weren't just tossing together word-salad. Each deals with the difficult, yet is up-lifting. Each chose a place and purpose for every word in relation to others–creating patterns in syntax that shape minds and hearts. These are places to explore another time.

For now, Orwell and Churchill (and Ricks) are calling to lighter and brighter, to enjoy.

October 21, 2021

The Next Thing?

"I wandered lonely as a cloud"
Daffodil flowers by ForestWander is licensed under CCA-SA-3.0 United States.
https://commons.wikimedia.org/wiki/File:Daffodil-Flowers_ForestWander.JPG

Who knows, with spring trying to make it in the northern hemisphere, and, for many months, nations that had leaders and populations enough with commonsense mostly Covid-clear, and opinion pollsters unable to excite us with poll results, and vaccinations seriously underway in many locations, perhaps we can feel okay reading Tolstoy, Jane Austen, Anthony Trollope, Muriel Spark, or whomever you prefer, unconcerned for now about any next black swan upsetting the millpond?

Maybe reflection, reminiscence, even nostalgia is permitted now? Just for a while, can we anticipate the tulips and daffodils, then savor the tastes and scents known only to the anxiety-free? Let the cat be the one leaping at shadows on the window.

Be relaxed, that book from 1999, *The New New Thing* is no longer on the best-seller list. Rest–[what a great word]–assured, we will be able to get through moments of Zen or other peace, and never miss that other dopamine, unexcited by the not-latest breaking news.

Weren't secret gardens dreamt up for this time? Why let politicians and other marketers of statistics make worry? Will you really lose your edge by taking a spring or summer break (dare we think?) away from the crowd? ...especially with skills gained from a year's lockdown!

Feel confident, someone will keep pots of potentiality stirred in your absence. Why let claptrap now rule your life when some lonely beach or wilderness holds such promise and might soon be enjoyed.

Let's hear it for this kind of *ennui!*

March 16, 2021

Honestly

Fishermen Unloading their Catch at the Pier at Portmagee
© Copyright Frank Donovan is licensed for reuse under
creativecommon.org/licenses/by-sa/2.0

Expected on full display off the coast of Ireland this week will be a contrast of values. With the deadly armaments of war-gamers potentially endangering Irish fishermen, it is real values and not pretense that will be clear to the world.

The war-gamers are set to fire naval artillery and rockets 150 miles off the Irish coast in international waters, but within the Irish exclusive economic zone (EEZ). Pat Murphy and his fellow fishermen have caught the attention of many worldwide, for promising to do what they've always done on the first of February–namely, work the fishing grounds off the coast of Ireland, from the start of the season.

What's clear already is that when Pat Murphy says he's not moving aside for war-gamers, you'd better believe it. He and a fellow fisherman made this known, armed only with maps of the fishing grounds, during a visit with the war-gamers' ambassador to Ireland.

Unsurprisingly, the two parties' readouts of this meeting, which were later given to the media, were different concerning a key undertaking—with the ambassador's public statement contradicting his private guarantee of safety given to Murphy. Mr. Murphy reportedly responded that he takes the ambassador's public comment as "a threat and an insult." As my Irish grandfather quipped more than once, there are no degrees of honesty.

As with most events of this type that involve devotees to war who are reported in the media, the slippery treatment of truth, half-truth, and myth will keep evolving as the coming week(s) unfold. This casual relationship with truth of warmongers, and war-gamers also it seems, was evident even before the first edition in 1975 of Phillip Knightley's revelatory *The First Casualty: The War Correspondent as Hero, Propagandist and Myth-Maker from the Crimea to Iraq*.

It's to be hoped the war-gamers might temporarily escape their own view of the world to know that an Irish fisherman named Pat Murphy will keep his word—he and his compatriots will be fishing and "not moving aside," when the war-gamers commence their dangerous maneuvers on Thursday, local time.

Just how many generations of Murphy families have fished off the Irish coast isn't clear. And which Murphy family would you be talking about, you might ask.

Population experts would likewise have a hard time guessing the scale of various extensions of the Murphy families and their countryfolk throughout the world. Estimates based on the rates with which Irish migrants in this country and elsewhere marry out of the Irish community, and extend the sharing of Irish values, would give some idea of this. Yet another clue could be the readership of books about Ireland, including *How the Irish Saved Civilization*—which tend to fly off the shelves of bookshops and libraries.

What the world is seeing many will consider a further repeat of what Sir Winston Churchill acknowledged as a "sorry history" of the Emerald Isle, so often subjected to intimidation and, in earlier times, invasion!

Whatever happens this week, many millions within and beyond Irish families, in a great many countries worldwide, will feel unity with Mr. Murphy and his fellow fishermen.

[FOOTNOTE UPDATE, February 1, 2022: *The Irish Echo* has reported "...the Russians have now said that they will relocate their naval exercises, though to exactly where is not clear. But they're not to be now staged in the Irish EEZ."]

January 30, 2022

Five Rings

Olympic Rings at the Top of Mount Takao
Anillos Olímpicos en la Cima del Monte Takao
by Antonio Tajuelo is licensed under CCA 2.0 Generic.
https://upload.wikimedia.org/wikipedia/commons/5/5d/Anillos_Ol%C3%ADmpicos_en_la_Cima_d
el_Monte_Takao_%2851146112701%29.jpg

The Olympic torch is once more passed forward. Beyond conception as the world's must-see platform for competitive sports excellence, the Olympic Games reliably deliver much more.

For the days of the competition and well beyond, the events put a spotlight on the best of human qualities, not only sports skill, strength, endurance, courage, and more, but popping up regularly too are occasions that showcase a human sense of fairness and grace, and care for strangers and friends drawn from so many parts of the world.

Little wonder then that we're ready to experience the modern Games, bringing together, as the rings symbolize, five of the world's inhabited continents, when considering North and South America as one–in a competitive spirit that expresses tremendous cooperation among peoples of these continents.

Perhaps the enthusiasts who, regularly in southern hemisphere summer, travel to the Antarctic to run a marathon will eventually find a way to help include this additional continent, with its too-little acknowledged 37 year-round scientific bases of non-permanent residents?

Against all impediments of difference, or dissent, or pandemic, a spirit of the ancient Olympics has passed forward for all of us, through generations of remarkable accomplishment by competitors, supporters, and organizers, well into our futures.

With Paralympians and the winter Games still to come, we can look forward to further reminders of some of the very best in people.

August 9, 2021

Vive Le Tour de France

Tour de France, Stage 5, Masny, 2022
TDF2022.Etape 5.peloton au sortir de Mans
by © Felouch Kotek is licensed under CCA 4.0 International.
https://upload.wikimedia.org/wikipedia/commons/1/1e/TDF2022_Et5.jpg

Le Tour 2022 commenced less than a week ago. Followers and fans on television or along roadways of the route will inhale a spectacle of cycling for more than a couple of weeks yet. Each nuance of tactic, tragedy, and triumph will be a shared experience.

For many years, veteran commentators Phil Liggett and the late Paul Sherwen personified the cyclists as "dancing on the pedals" or "reaching into a suitcase of courage"–their words immortalizing the human struggle that's played out on the race route through the European landscapes of villages, architecture, ancient and newer cities, mountains, and bucolic countryside.

Le Tour puts a spotlight on fitness, endurance, courage, skill, ingenuity, competition, cooperation, camaraderie, and more, while sharing a fascination of human beings with visual spectacle. We can all recall scenes or occasions that capture our attention or imagination. Many remain sharply in our memory. It's a natural inclination of human beings to think visually.

What catches attention or what we think important (visually or otherwise) we'll even say is "top of mind" or "front of mind." It might be our very own "red, red rose" or "road not taken" that will take shape as the image we see, but it will be a *red rose* or a *road*.

We frequently use the visual power of a variety of words for readers and listeners to see people, creatures, actions, places, objects, colors, shapes, events, processes, concepts, and other "stuff" not on this list. And the *visual words* we choose can also infer how we think about or experience other senses.

Each time the leading teams of cyclists and the peloton whisk along their winding pathways of history, I recall the fortresses on hilltops across France, blown up on Richelieu's orders to centralize the power of the monarchy, through to 160 years later "the mob tearing down, stone by stone, the hated fortress-prison at what remains in today's Paris as the name, *Place de la Bastille*" (Bradbury, p. 38)–bookmarking the beginnings and the close of France's literary Golden Age of the Enlightenment, and the foundation of the Republic.

Each year *Le Tour* emerges on the calendar as three weeks of anticipated spectacle and provides a visual experience that reliably floods memory with the significance of France's contributions to Western civilization–especially the evolution of a worldwide commitment of free peoples to give expression to **Liberté, égalité,** and **fraternité.**

July 5, 2022

Beyond Reason

Depressione
by Aurora Mazzoldi w:it.Aurora_Mazzoldi is licensed under CCA-SA-3.0 Unported.
https://commons.wikimedia.org/wiki/File:Depressione.jpg

As the inexorable grind of the United States legal processes progress in the coming months and years, accountability for words will come into even sharper focus.

Scrutiny of the gossip-sphere of social media might finally see some requirements for reasonable behavior beyond the user agreements of social media companies that this week proved to be valuable for now.

Capitol rioters are about to discover in court how sophisticated the tools of law enforcement have become during recent decades to detect bad behavior online, before and after mob violence.

Skilled analyses of the public and dark webs, assembling evidence of involvement and intent, are just some of the tools that are now routine in much law enforcement. Two decades of efforts to anticipate the intent of terrorists, by analyzing behavior and language, have delivered many advances in detecting intent.

The tools of language analysis to attribute authorship from relatively small samples of text are also much more refined. Stylometry techniques commenced almost 100 years ago have developed further from 50 years ago in Sweden and Britain to arbitrate the authorship of plays by Shakespeare, Fletcher, Marlowe, and Middleton. Almost 40 years ago, I used stylistic analysis of language to advise the Director of Public Prosecutions on the likely authorship of an accused murderer's disputed police record of interview.

Public language such as the positive-sounding codewords used to incite mobs are appropriate for legal attention too. We all know what "Fight like hell" means in the context of a mob and riot; accumulated positive-sounding codewords, extolling the coming utopia, are not any more neutral in context and are easy to track because of their repetition.

Of course, so many criminals seem driven by belief in their own superiority that the "knock at their door" by law enforcement in coming days, weeks, months, or even years will likely still be a surprise.

January 13, 2021

Making It So

Mountain Bluebird
Sialia currucoides by Elaine R. Wilson is licensed under CCA-SA 2.5 Generic.
https://upload.wikimedia.org/wikipedia/commons/0/03/Mountain_Bluebird.jpg

You are

to the violin

as a bee

to the flower,

bringing continuous life

to spring.

Perhaps also honoring this violinist's virtuoso performance from a time before Covid-19, in the early morning today, full-throated chirrups and calls floated through the open window, making another springtime symphony.

These performances fittingly commemorate on Memorial Day the many who gave all, to provide opportunity for life, liberty, and the pursuit of happiness to each of us.

In an effort to sustain such commitment going forward, almost eighty-one years ago during the bleak beginnings to World War II, Roosevelt and Churchill agreed the Atlantic Charter—interestingly, never signed yet continuously honored—and ever since serving as a foundation for ongoing alliance of democracies against autocratic rivals.

With this bond "updated" and reaffirmed on June 10 in 2021, both Britain and the United States agreed to adhere to "the rules-based international order," focus on the "climate crisis," and "protect biodiversity"—as well as calling on Western Allies to "oppose interference through disinformation or other malign influences, including in elections."

The New York Times described this as "an effort to stake out a grand vision for global relationships in the 21st century." Unquestionably, and as irrepressible as this morning's symphony, it also reaffirmed commitment for the liberties of thought, speech, and association to continuously grow.

Once experienced, nothing else will do.

May 30, 2022

Votes for Action

Bald Eagle (Haliaeetus leucocephalus)
About to Launch, (Kachemak Bay, Alaska) by Andy Morffew, CCA-BY-2.0 Generic.
https://commons.wikimedia.org/w/index.php?curid=61980497

In the past week, enough voters who identify as Independent or Republican have joined Democrats to bolster democracy in the United States, importantly with projected control of the Senate–in what might prove to be one of the largest positive counters to a "propaganda of the deed" (Bolt, pp. 3-21).

Not that perpetrators of violence or blathering threats in the name of pseudo-populism will "just disappear," any more than other social sicknesses do. Still required is further action for accountability.

Yet this midterm election has delivered important positives, not least a rebuke to the "anti-" behaviors megaphoned at us all for far too long.

A coalition of voters expressed a "roar" which, for the moment, drowns out screams for the camera. Voters reasserted the ideals on which the

United States of America was founded—right back at the incessant nattering of recast "nabobs of negativity," who were rejected as nihilists and exploiters of the democratic system.

Less than one week along, with counting of votes continuing, what's sinking in is the significance. Some historians call this the best midterm election result for an incumbent party and first-term president in at least 60 years. The election result surely reaffirms many Americans' faith in "we the people."

Election workers, whistleblowers, local officials, journalists, and many more people in the United States have shown resilience against the ongoing propaganda of violence, screamed threats, and character assassination—enabling voters to speak out.

A strengthened faith of a people in their countryfolk is being echoed by more in the media. Can we hope fertile seeds are sown for more than a reprieve from a dark alternative?

November 13, 2022

Humor

What's So Funny?

"A horse is tied to a 10 minute parking sign" by Charles Edward is licensed under CCA-SA3.0 Unported.
https://commons.wikimedia.org/wiki/File:A_horse_tied_to_a_10_minute_parking_sign_at_the_battle_of_Corydon_reenactment.JPG

A delightful book on *The Language of Humour* by Walter Nash just arrived in the mail. Worth every penny on the second-hand market, if you're prepared to risk never smiling again, after reading Nash's analyses of the joke, anecdote, pun, parody, humorous rhythms, overstatement / understatement / counterstatement, and all manner of funny-bone ticklers in-between.

My reward for buying second-hand, however, was at the cost of some next generations of students at Villanova University in Philadelphia no longer having access to the humor and its principles in this slim book on their library shelf—as the stamp "NO LONGER PROPERTY OF..." that a librarian there in search of more shelf-space was obliged to announce inside the front cover.

Why this book is interesting is that for all the wonderful humor that keeps the world healthy and for all the descriptions of the effects of humor, we are less well served with explanation of the causes of humor. For some of the more intelligent speculations about why we laugh, we must go back to French philosopher, Henri Bergson, writing in 1900. He described his purpose in exploring humor as better understanding what it is to be human. He talked about many aspects, including the social role of laughter, the part played by exaggeration of human features, gesture and movements, and the relationship of the comic to human imagination.

Walter Nash's book is packed with a mix of examples of humor of course. One of the more famous being the restaurant diner asking, "Waiter, what's this fly doing in my soup?" for the waiter's reply, "Looks like the breast-stroke, sir."–as an example of the *pragmatic factor*. Or an example of the bizarre *pun*, "What do you do with a wombat?–Play wom." In the interests of space, these are among the shorter samples.

The value of the book is not so much the examples, as the attempt at outlining some principles. Although published in 1985, for today's readers there might be too many historical (and not even hysterical) examples that relied on sexism or other appeals now considered inappropriate. Maybe this was the reason for my copy's removal from the university library's shelf? Another limitation of the book is that it could do with more examples not so literary or Anglo-centric. Still, with so little of worth looking at humor, which is an elixir for so many of us sharing emailed jollies at this bizarre time, Nash's book is worth a look–if, like Bergson, you're interested in an important aspect of what makes us human.

One commentator on political humor, whom I read recently, suggested that a universal theory of humor is yet to be developed that takes into consideration three major theories, namely superiority, relief, and incongruity. What's clear is that the human emotions behind humor remain a bit of a mystery and complex. Perhaps that's why at this time that the talk of public figures is so rife with blatant banality, plus insult and injury of **we the people;** with some so lacking in empathy or other emotions we value, that we hear little or no humor from them. Among politicians, who do you remember last able to make us laugh at all, much less for the right reasons?

August 6, 2020

Fabulists

Initiale E. Lune, montagne, et reflet dans un lac
This image from "Songs of a Sentimental Bloke," p. 64, 1916 edition
is in the Public Domain {{PD-US-expired}}
https://commons.wikimedia.org/wiki/File:Songs_of_a_sentimental_bloke_p._63_initial.svg

It's just as well dictionaries pay no heed to the principle of guilt by association. Otherwise, literature's long line of fabulists would be lumped in with a second sense of the word, as "liars." [namely, "FABLE MAKER" both: "1. composer of fables" AND "2. teller of tales; a liar."]

Certainly, Aesop, Brothers Grimm, Hans Christian Andersen, Jean De La Fontaine through George Orwell and James Thurber, and many others do make stuff up. But fable writers delight us with truths, for young readers through many much older—with tales like *The Tortoise and the Hare*, *The Ugly Duckling* or, more recently, the extended fairytales of *Animal Farm* and *The Wonderful O*.

Thank goodness for the charm of tales that spotlight a moral, or offer other enlightenment, or humor, or hope. Quite a contrast to some torturous, terror-filled taletellers today, especially the barbaric and wannabe tyrants who fill the airwaves with lies.

Nasties like these get their comeuppance though, when James Thurber amusingly explores in one of his fantasies, titled *The Wonderful O,* their theft of the letter "O." Thanks to someone in Oxford taking the trouble to count the occurrence of letters, we can know that the letter "O" is 37-times more generally used than the letter "Q" in English. So, the effect on people's communication in Thurber's fantasy kingdom is severe. And he takes readers delightfully through the difficulties and disruptions that the theft of "O" causes, as well as what happens [deleted spoiler alert] to that kingdom's thieving tyrants.

Just as well Thurber's nasties didn't steal the letter "E" of course, which the diligent Oxonian says is our favorite letter to use, at 57-times more than the letter "Q." It's also the most common letter in Czech, Danish, Dutch, French, German, Hungarian, Latin, Latvian, Norwegian, Spanish, Swedish, and some other languages. To see how challenging it would be to live with that theft, I had a go writing a tale not using our most popular letter. Writing as if a thief had won by stealing away use of the letter "E," the tale started like this:

> **In a land** not far away, in which birds roar and big cats sing, it is an *Almost-KING* who's ranting about what's what. Occasional pundits still parrot *His* almost-royal trash-talk, using what I think of as bigly words, or not, again, again, again, and again. Within this land now, all living things, or humans anyway, must cast a ballot to outlaw anything that's not what our *Almost-KING* calls "what," such as voting to ban or burn books–or, if you avoid voting, you must pay fifty dollars to the *Almost-Royal Fund*. With topsy also almost turvy, what's up is down and what is, is not..."

The first and only review (by my wife) of an earlier, longer version of this e-deficient tale was that she didn't know what on earth this meant. I'm guessing more was missing than just the familiar letter, "**E.**" But give it a try yourself, if you like... not so nice to live without our favorite letter, eh?

29

Yet with that temporary **E**-drought broken for now, how should we feel about democracy denialists, who want us to live without effective use for FR' 'DOM..., with it's two too many ee's? Of course, much more to lose with that theft... much more.

So, you've doubtless got the drift of Thurber's little book, *The Wonderful O,* which is more than totally worth the read–and it's an especially recommended read for THIS MONTH.

Oh, and please vote! Otherwise, just imagine the consequence of this being the last Halloween, just because that children's celebration clearly has too many **ee**'s.

Amid the furore of such a theft, who'd even notice the departure of Milton's *Paradise Lost.* Oh yes, also, do I need to mention to make a memo to self that freedom is on the ballot too?!

And can you get others, who care, to VOTE? Or, as Sesame Street foretold, we're all in the hands of the Cookie Monster [2 minute video, below]. For **eeee**'s sake.

Note

Sesame Street (2002), *Cookie's Letter of the Day E,*
   https://archive.org/details/videoplayback-2021-09-06-t-101937.912

October 18, 2022

Humor-in-Law

1955 Austin A30
by Vauxford is licensed under CCA-SA 4.0 International.
https://commons.wikimedia.org/wiki/File:1955_Austin_A30_Seven_800cc.jpg

Studying criminal law way back when, a required class assignment was to provide a full report on a court proceeding. Finding a case to audit was probably part of the test, since this required locating the right noticeboard in the old courthouse downtown, firstly to choose from the list of hearings for the day, then to navigate the musty corridors of the old courthouse building, to be in the right place at the right time.

And this also turned out to be an early and unexpected experience of humor-in-law, before television audiences enjoyed the now dated but legendary British comedy series, *Rumpole of the Bailey*.

The case I happened to choose was the preliminary hearing of three accused men, caught after a bank robbery gone wrong. The getaway car was an Austin A30, well-known in British Commonwealth countries at the time as an old family sedan, commonly referred to as a "baby Austin," not noted for speed.

The tip-off to the arresting police was the car's license plate on the rear of the car, observed to be dangling vertically, just held by one shoelace;

with the second shoelace that had kept this license plate horizontal and in place no longer visible, having surrendered its duty somewhere in the hurly-burly of getting away from the bank.

Revealed to the police, firmly affixed, horizontal, and easily read underneath was the original license plate of this stolen car. So, the police pulled the baby Austin to the side of the road on suspicion, and the jig was up when pistols and canvas bags of bank money were sighted.

With these facts, like a scene from Gilbert and Sullivan or another farce, it only occasionally gets any better when studying law! Not sure how the presiding magistrate kept a straight face as the prosecutor outlined each piece of evidence.

Equally remarkable was the dialog that occurred during recesses in the morning's proceedings, when the magistrate was not present. The police prosecutor and the accused men evidenced almost back-slapping "friendliness," apparently well-known to each other—with other police in the courtroom smiling discretely, appreciating these exchanges. Unsurprisingly, the prosecutor was optimistic about bringing a case to finally secure the three accused for a time, at Her Majesty's pleasure.

The defense lawyer was more braggadocious in retelling, to anyone who'd listen, titbits of conversations he'd had with his clients during their dinners at his home; he was a big talker, combining poor dress sense with a diamond ring on one hand, and with a slickness just a touch akin to the character of the lawyer, Vinny, in the movie *My Cousin Vinny*. Yet he lacked most of the smarts of the movie lawyer.

After these proceedings, I didn't track the outcome of the trial or any appeals; time to follow that progress was required for other assignments and, in those days, would also have required continuous checking of the right noticeboard in the courthouse; but it didn't look too promising for the three accused men during this preliminary hearing, which resulted in a clear case to answer.

Updating to the present in the United States, some of the more than 500 cases in progress against the January 6 terrorists at the Capitol present facts strangely similar. The terrorists' plans were large, but disconnected, and flawed enough in execution to permit over 300 million Americans to dodge, for now, the intended result of some 9,000 terrorists, who injured about 140 police while attempting to violently overturn democratic government. Many behaviors of the terrorists were as bizarre and darkly comedic as those of the bank robbers.

Of course, anyone facing armed attackers, whether bank robbers or terrorists, with life put at risk, sees no humor. Bizarre as these events look in the rear-view mirror, they're a stark reminder of the importance to anticipate, pursue, and prosecute criminals soonest and well.

Dumb luck is a fickle ally.

September 1, 2021

Cows & Curtains

Thirsty wallaby on a Queensland Property
by W. Matthewson & State Library of Queensland
is in the Public Domain {{PD-US-expired}}
https://commons.wikimedia.org/wiki/File:
Thirsty_wallaby_on_a_Queensland_property_(5184026012).jpg

How delightful that we gained another hour of light at the end of today, thanks to "falling back" from Daylight Saving Time, in the United States anyway.

This bonus from frugality is a treat, especially if you've suffered through endless public wrangles sometime about the merits, or not, of setting the clocks forward in the spring–to enable such generosity for this day in the fall. Tussles over the terrors of time adjustment can tear at local communities–some call theft what others call a gift of extra sunlight, to play or get extra chores done in daylight. Everyone seems to have an opinion. In an early local debate in Australia, one of the louder advocates for not messing with *Tempus Fugit* was a politician who, as a former farmer, knew a thing or two about messing with "rules of nature." He was very knowledgeable, he said, about when the cows expect to be milked!!

Amid others' commentaries were when children needed afternoon snacks after school, and, of course, the extra hour of tropical sunlight would fade the curtains. You think I'm making this up? 'fraid not–perhaps you heard equally preposterous polemic pressing panic buttons locally in your community (but hopefully not).

During deliberations on so momentous a proposition, the media generously sustains ever-prescient insights about the pros and cons, seeking to elevate each skirmish of the debate into a gladiatorial battle. Rarely was so much expended by so many about so little, as for the potential losses and gains from adjusting just sixty minutes. And thankfully some playful commentators added parody and humorous quips to the debate.

This raging public discourse for the politician was, of course, more than harmless diversion. It was just one more of the many mock controversies he stoked. His polemic helped distract attention and energy from dismantling the gerrymanders and electoral malapportionment he'd quietly installed.

Sounding familar?

Frequently he was re-elected with a smaller number of votes than the state's two other major parties. He kept his leadership and his political party in power in coalition with one of the other parties–benefiting also from a preferential voting system. He maneuvered this with about 20 to 27% of the primary vote for five elections before defeating the "coalition party" decisively in two more elections. All this and more kept him in the driver's seat for almost 20 years.

Unfortunately, today's time adjustment doesn't provide an extra hour for voting on Tuesday... so, best plan now, which five people–neighbors, family, friends–you can help get to a voting booth (where this is still permitted by state law!!), to cast votes in the poll that matters.

November 6, 2022

When Fools Rule

Make Way for Ducklings Prank, Boston Common
Sign warns: No photographs to avoid erosion from the light emitted by cameraphones. "An April Fools' Day prank…" by Whoisjohngalt is licensed under CCA-BY-SA 3.0 Unported.
https://commons.wikimedia.org/wiki/File:Make_Way_For_Ducklings_Prank.jpg

Once the glory day for pranksters, April Fools' Day seems to be less dutifully observed these days. Sometimes the pranks are good-humored, harmless, and funny. Unfortunately, some cause an injury to feelings at least. Perhaps any decline in this second type might be welcomed as a change to human nature. Are we now less inclined to find humor in the distress of others? Let's hope any injury is modest enough to easily forgive and soon forget.

Some April Fools' pranks live longer than others though. One radio broadcaster when I was growing up, appropriately and affectionately known to his listeners as "Bird Brain Bert Robertson," caught the wrath of city officials one April 1st. He told his listeners that the city would soon turn off the water supply to all suburbs. He so convincingly urged his large group of loyal listeners to get prepared for their day's domestic water needs by filling buckets, pots, sinks, and bathtubs, that the City Water Commissioner asked Bird Brain to stop at once; the level of water in the Dam supplying the city was dramatically falling.

When Bird Brain informed listeners of their April foolishness, they delighted in his offbeat success and quickly forgave him. Regardless of the wasted water, for which he'd not be so readily forgiven today, the effect then was that Bird Brain's popularity rose further. These days, a NOT-forgivable prank too often played out any day of the year is by some "bird brain" politician who dreams up outrage to get a headline.

As my grandmother would have said, tarred with the same brush, and even less forgivable is the media sub-editor who publishes the outrage [even if critical of it–please see other blog posts on the uselessness of "not" and so-called fact-checking]. And, LESS forgivable because the media sub-editor sets an expectation in journalists that "we the people" are willing to still be the victims of the sickness in those outrage pranks of a politician.

Little wonder that the residual effect of such foolishness in public communication is an appetite among some media gatekeepers for more foolish fiction. I guess this was what caused journalists to turn up recently to their first press conference with a new President to put questions with in-built potential to manufacture outrage.

These journalists' questions sounded eerily like they were distilled from partisan talking points; which themselves result from questions that media-manipulators put to members of focus groups to stimulate pre-determined foolishness. Anyone who doesn't see this as truly bizarre, even without the other bizarre truth that political parties, media, and other companies pay money to support this whole set-up, needs at least another cup of coffee.

Also, little wonder then, that this charade of ever-increasing competition for media listeners is causing so many of us to find and enjoy other pursuits. It's remarkable that such a tragicomedy continues–a relic of a bye-gone era that was itself manufactured by media rating agencies.

Someone should point out that the world has changed.

April 1, 2021

Leadership

Homage

Cattle Graze in an Iowa Field
by Preston Keres/US Dept of Agriculture.
This image is in the Public Domain {{PD-USGov}}
https://commons.wikimedia.org/wiki/File:20170913-FAS-PJK-4328_TONED_(37224822395).jpg

George Orwell concluded his *Homage to Catalonia* with a reflection on his return to England, "earthquakes in Japan, famines in China, revolutions in Mexico... [the people] ...all sleeping the deep, deep sleep of England… [will be] …jerked out of it by the roar of bombs."

This was 1937, when Orwell returned from a harrowing time as a volunteer in the fight against fascists, during the Spanish War. Although it's not possible now to know just how, greater efforts at that time to weaken or defeat the fascists could have seen events from 1939 onwards unfold very differently.

It was not only England that was sleeping. Throughout a world still slowly recovering from a Great Depression, in rural areas, cities, and towns, people on farms and in offices and factories sought peace of mind for a better life–while leaders of the Axis Powers secretly made massive preparations for conquest.

Their first forays with bombs and troops were to take control of countries as staging areas for further conquest.

The world waited and watched from elsewhere, until the disparate and distracting debates increasingly presented by members of the Fifth Column telling smart-sounding lies could no longer shield elected representatives from the duty to protect homelands. Compelled by overwhelming circumstances, people worldwide progressively woke from sleep, to harrowing years of action.

Foremost among what was different then was that Hitler, from very early, so completely lied about his intentions.

March 5, 2022

Neighbors

Napoleon in Exile at St Helena
Helen Leah Reed. This image is in the Public Domain {{PD-US-expired}}
https://commons.wikimedia.org/wiki/File:Napoleon_at_St._Helena.jpg

Much like family, we don't usually get to pick our neighbors. Pleasant times spent with a neighbor chatting and sharing stories, drinks, or a meal provide a sense of belonging, security, and peace of mind within immediate and familiar surroundings—extending the valued bubble of comfort and security of home that anyone should be able to expect.

Some neighbors become life-long friends. Some take on the care of houseplants or pets when we travel. Looking out for each other and caring about someone else are good qualities in folks we'd call good neighbors.

Of course, in different ways tough on everyone are those neighbors only interested in themselves. Least troublesome are the ones who keep to themselves. But the one or two who dispute the fence-line, push too much, or make a lot of noise or worse are the flip side.

More widely in the world they're often mocked or illustrative of what's ridiculous but dangerous, frighteningly real compared to the cartoon characters their actions prompt.

I recall a Donald Duck cartoon strip in which Donald got his feathers so greatly in a flap with his neighbor that they each frantically built fences higher and higher on their adjacent fence-line, to outdo each other.

Eventually, the fences were many times higher than their homes, bending and swaying from the height of the fences that Donald and his neighbor were atop and still building, when the cartoonist summoned a tornado to whisk both fences away onto a nearby body of water—there to serve as life-rafts for passengers escaping a ferry that was overturned by the same tornado—such is the power of the cartoonist's pen to find a good ending to madness.

The longer that dangerous actions are allowed, the greater the harm for everyone.

February 21, 2022

Thylacine

Thylacinus cynocephalus, 1863
by John Gould (1804-1881) & Henry Constantine Richter (1821-1902), *Mammals of Australia*, Vol 1 Plate 54. This image is in the Public Domain {{PD-US-expired}}
https://commons.wikimedia.org/wiki/File:Thylacinus_cynocephalus_(Gould).jpg

No longer seen and mostly under-appreciated was Thylacine, commonly known as the Tasmanian Tiger because of its striped lower back.

Since this carnivore ceased to roam the islands of Tasmania and New Guinea, and the Australian mainland, its continuing claims to fame include supporting the official coat of arms for the State of Tasmania, being appropriated on a beer label, and, more recently, featuring as a character in a video game.

This presumed extinct marsupial is sometimes confused with a different marsupial, popularized by the Looney Tunes cartoon as the whirling carnivore, the Tasmanian Devil. However, Thylacine was not equipped for high speed running, and could briefly do a hop on hind legs, a bit like a kangaroo.

It's a stretch to draw much comparison with William Blake's description of the Asian "tyger's... fearful symmetry," since, according to

Wikipedia, Thylacine was known in the wild and in captivity just to growl and hiss when agitated, exhibit a threat-yawn, and when hunting gave rapidly repeated guttural cough-like barks.

Unambiguously a predator though, it was able to open its jaws to an unusual extent, and likely relied on sight and sound in its nocturnal hunting, mainly of large ground-dwelling birds. The decline in population of these birds, resulting from human hunting of the same birds, might have correlated with the demise of the Thylacine in the wild.

Despite the doubts that scientists have expressed more recently about the strength of Thylacine's jaws to deal with more than the light bones found in birds and smaller animals, rumors occurred in earlier times about the Tasmanian Tiger attacking sheep. In any case, the fate of this interesting and extinct creature seems to confirm Thomas Hobbes's relativities of life in nature as "nasty, brutish, and short," especially if competing with human beings.

Growing up in Australia, my reading included the weekly Nature Notes in a local newspaper by David Fleay, whose legacy included creating one of the few movie-clips we have of this extinct animal. Thanks to the life-long efforts of trailblazers like Fleay, who first bred the Platypus and other native species and developed initiatives to protect endangered species, what people can do individually and collectively to advance such efforts is now more in the spotlight.

Which puts perspective on public communication more broadly today. Amid the endless articles and books that review the last five years of America's political decay, a nagging concern is that even the best of these do little more than uncover malign activity—and put a laser focus on diagnosis.

Journalists and pundits, in the United States at least, reveal the disaster that's continuing like a cancer, eating away at the democratic system in unsubtle ways. The open question remains who will address treatment regimens? Where are today's Orwell and Ellul to point the way to remedy?

Where are the young, savvy individuals who have the chops to execute needed change?

As both education and the vote became more generally available over recent centuries, regrettably almost in parallel, educational curricula jettisoned the teaching of grammar, dialectics, and rhetoric to make room for many educators' pet and sometimes important subjects. Dorothy Sayers highlighted this trend as commencing well before her 1947 address to a Vacation Course in Education at Oxford, which was later published as *The Lost Tools of Learning*.

Recent generations were sometimes able to remedy their schooling's neglect of English grammar through later study of Latin, French, or other languages, but mostly had to rely on self-education for logic, or smatterings of dialectics and rhetoric. As a result of this myopia in education, as Sayers noted, the ability to differentiate "fact from opinion and the proven from the plausible" declined.

It's unsurprising then, that the misinformation we are living through includes what some journalists and pundits so gratuitously and erroneously propagate and bemoan as a "lack of bipartisanship." This ready catch cry often props up a media report–and misses the point.

Regrettably, in the United States and it seems in other places around the world, what we now have, and ought to vigorously address in every way possible, is better described as "null-partisan politics" or more simply, "monolog." Masquerading as populism, its devotees are nearest to anarchists or nihilists in ideology, with primary commitment to self.

It's time to call out occasions that pose as debate but are about nullifying civil society. When talk occurs at a tangent to addressing the public good, whether or not it's manufactured outrage, it offers nothing useful to society; it is monolog and should be shown to be. This absurdity of public communication needs dismantling and disentangling from its pretense as debate. The continuing reality seems to be that the monolog vacuum of "NO" is what we hear in response to proposed initiatives to address people's needs.

It requires creativity to expect better and to call on the vacuous to do better. It's more than time to spotlight this sad scene in our public communication—which, in some ways, is akin to when one child goes to a playground and is only able to sit alone and immobilized on one end of a seesaw, because no one else turns up to sit on the other end of the seesaw.

Too many elected representatives now seem to believe that the role of each individual elected member is to clamor for their own monolog on the media (a very 70s and 80s concept of public relations, if ever a useful activity), keen to be on any TV, or radio, or podcast, or social media, often in tandem with propagating slurs and rumors. And, a wide variety of partisan or not-so-partisan media oblige, spreading sometimes wildly dangerous fantasies, as if this constitutes news or is otherwise of interest.

Will we ever see social media and other media satisfactorily self- or otherwise regulated to take responsibility for content seriously? Will we ever see educational systems that sufficiently prepare new generations with the abilities needed to discern, analyze, criticize, and synthesize reality?

So, taking the fate of the Tasmanian Tiger as analogy, if you'd like a future that's better than just being a memory within a coat of arms, beer label, or video game, best get prepared for the wilds of no-debate land—a Wild West where the norms that rule are drawn from anachronisms like the rancher's open range and pitiful imitations of the Marlboro Man.

November 1, 2021

Go High

Isocrates (436-338 BC)
"Rhetoric as that endowment of our human nature which raises us... to live the civilized life."
by Student Vives TVW is licensed under CCA-SA-4.0 International.
https://commons.wikimedia.org/wiki/File:Afbeelding_van_Isocrates..jpg

During this never quiet time in the Silly Season of another election, you might find some renewal in checking out Philip Collins's thoughts about Speeches that Shape the World and Why We Need Them–this is the subtitle for his book titled *When They Go Low, We Go High*.

After the launch of this book, in which Collins of course discusses the source of its title, Sam Leith put a microphone in front of the author for *The Spectator podcast* on 25 October 2017. Early in this interesting interview, Collins points out that the best case for democracy is what it prevents, as Albert Camus had noted.

Collins goes further in his book, comparing democracy and populist utopia (pp. 71-84). This emphasizes again for me the wisdom of keeping close with people who know how little they know.

If someone also aims for the stars while keeping feet on the ground, then you've likely found a true leader. The true leader shares feelings for what "we the people" care about; and talks with us to let us know what the leader will do to:

* Help **put a roof overhead** and keep it there.

* See we can get **food**.

* Assure **health care** we can afford.

* Provide a pathway to a **job**.

* Respect our **freedoms** and **peace of mind**.

For this person, the Universal Declaration of Human Rights will be a governing principle. These are just some of the ways we can "go high."

Collins's book focuses mainly on speeches that address these very real concerns of any of us. The speeches that he discusses are, in my opinion, mainly Good (Pericles, Lincoln, Pankhurst, Churchill, Kennedy, Mandala, King, Reagan, etc.), with a few of the Bad and Ugly (Hitler, Castro, Mao), along with a host of others worthy of attention.

With his insider's understanding as a former prime ministerial speechwriter in Britain, Collins shares lesser known insights about the context, composition, and delivery of the speeches. He has put together an entertaining read. In both podcast and book, he points out the virtues of going high, to change people's circumstances for the better, through politics.

He also shares some interestingly common "tells" about the autocrats. They consistently self-indulge how poorly-done-by they are, especially by the media not loving them—and are forever angry. Sound familiar? And their utopia ordinarily requires returning to some mythically better past; seemingly unable to show us a better future, much less to do so with humor.

Another well-known commonality of autocrats, Collins writes, is to drumbeat various inventions about conspiracies of the elite against the people; consistently claiming that "utopia [is] just around the corner, if only the corrupt elite had cared to venture there." Another tell is that the propagandist/autocrat self-portrays as leading efforts to "rise above the smears, and ludicrous slanders from ludicrous reporters." Yet another tell is to claim, "a lot of people are saying," as authority for some preposterous drivel. It appears this is all in every days' "work" for the self-dealing autocrat.

Collins's book is a worthwhile and reassuring read at this time. Engagingly brief also is his description of rhetoric as a positive, developed canon of principle and knowledge. This addresses my pet peeve about the educators or others who preface their analyses of propaganda with long preachy explanations of rhetoric. Please, would you put your energy and words toward the better use of rhetoric's tools of analysis that have been around for some 2,400 years.

How about we all do what we can to nudge the understanding of rhetoric, as other than a pejorative, into the popular imagination and, as a system for living, back into the mainstream of all educational curricula!

Maybe then the vain regrets about *The Lost Tools of Learning,* in a booklet published in Oxford in 1948, would actually go to some purpose. Maybe then, just maybe a propagandist wouldn't have such an unchecked path.

Maybe a propagandist could be caught out and stopped in time in future.

October 15, 2020

"Aotearoa"

The Remarkables Reflected in Lake Wakatipu
Queenstown, New Zealand
Nick Bramhall, Wikimedia Commons CC BY-SA 2.0 Generic.
https://commons.wikimedia.org/wiki/File:The_Remarkables_(1126885451).jpg

… is often translated from the Māori to describe New Zealand as the "land of the long white cloud."

Although New Zealanders see the unwelcome pall of Covid-19 drifting away for now, they might feel a bit like their All Blacks rugby team just after many a match—elated at a win and yet to recover from the effort.

First Sunrise

Alternate translations of *Aotearoa* are "long bright world" or "land of abiding day."

As a recent writer for *Politico* put it, "the first major country to see the sun rise every day may also be the first to get a good look at life after Covid-19."

A Leader Matters

Certainly, the decisive statements and actions of Prime Minister Ardern seemed to do the trick, expecting the best of New Zealanders, who delivered.

Some observers, lacking much in the way of recent experiences of this, found quite remarkable what happens when you can trust your government.

Whatever quibbles or more that the future brings as we learn more about this virus, what we learned for now and then is that a leader can matter to head off mass suffering.

People Matter Too

In some other countries, I'm just hoping that a version of Leo Tolstoy's thoughts on great military leadership results.

At the close of *War and Peace,* he claims great military successes result from something like an infectious collective action among the troops, in concert with unfolding events, rather than any great value in what a leader says or does.

In many places, with medical staff, other first responders, state governors, local officials, and individuals increasingly taking actions that are often complementary, thankfully it's starting to look like Tolstoy was on to something.

The "troops," that is, local **leaders, workers and other citizens are making progress**.

May 19, 2020

Face Up to Absurdity

Facing the absurd—"Vae Victus"
by Arthur Szyk (1894-1951) is licensed under CC-BY-SA-4.0 International.
https://commons.wikimedia.org/wiki/File:Arthur_Szyk_(1894-1951)._Anti-Christ_(1942),_New_York.jpg

With each passing day, the absurd harm to lives and livelihood worldwide from the Covid-19 pandemic continues with little check.

How leaders of countries, regions, and localities protect citizens will be long remembered. Now is the time to call out the added absurdity of any leader's behavior deserving to be called out–and to keep calling it out.

Intriguing Discussion

Ongoing events remind me of an intriguing discussion with the man credited to first describe the theater of the absurd. Decades ago, when I called Stanford University's "communication group" to seek an appointment with an appropriate faculty member, I was directed to Martin Esslin.

The authority on the theater of the absurd, who had coined this term, Esslin had just returned to serve as professor of drama. He graciously welcomed a visit, with the length of the visit stretching as he probed my interest in propaganda.

He shared insights on his work after 1943, when he had participated in counter-propaganda radio broadcasts. This was for the British propaganda broadcaster during World War II that pretended to be a radio station of the German military broadcasting network.

The Nazis required people in occupied countries to listen only to German radio broadcasts. After the broadcast of Hitler's speeches, Esslin and others from the BBC would broadcast in German an immediate analysis of his speeches that was unfavorable to the Germans.

Dealing with the Absurd

I have ever since wondered how much Esslin's time in this involvement impacted his later critical thinking to describe the theater of the absurd. He was keen that I shift my Master of Arts research to focus on the radio station's files, which he believed were still untouched at the BBC archives. He was prepared to facilitate my access for a study that he felt could be groundbreaking.

It was intriguing and wonderful advice that I was too young in perspective or wisdom to follow. The project might have defined a different personal future. Instead, I returned to Australia to pursue other initiatives which were life-changing in other ways.

To Defeat a Bad Actor

An enduring lesson from this discussion with Esslin is the extraordinary effort needed to **face and defeat an unfit leader.**

May 24, 2020

Tales of Two

Auckland Islands, Looking towards New Zealand
Cape Lovitt by Lawrie Mead (LawrieM)&Tony Nicklin. This image is in the Public Domain.
https://commons.wikimedia.org/wiki/File:Cape_Lovitt.JPG

Joan Druett in *Island of the Lost* brings to life the character of people who, sailing into forbidding seas, were shipwrecked on a remote island 285 miles to the south of New Zealand. She recounts how two groups deal with deprivation at the "edge of the world" in the year 1864–as current today as then. The tales reveal the best and most base in humanity–starkly contrasting adaptability and rigidity in the respective leaders of the groups. One group showed courage in selfless acts too many to know, a flexibility in fighting overwhelming forces, and a determination to survive–qualities largely lacking in the second group.

Part history and part immersion in human nature, the author finds her stride early to bring to life the events and voices of the individuals, through her carefully creative interpretation of journals and other research. She relates the true tales of two groups, who were castaway and unaware of each other's existence, at different ends of the same island. Each took a different approach to making decisions and to finding shelter or food—with consequently different outcomes. Powerful recreations of ships, sea, storms, islands, vegetation, sea lions, birdlife, and other creatures are described in graphic detail, along with the cruelty needed to survive. Druett melds seamlessly the records of events within descriptions of the island setting, illustrating how castaways cope, insightfully sharing thoughts and actions of people facing extreme challenges to their lives.

The smaller group of castaways celebrate human savvy in undertaking hard efforts, using limited tools retrieved from their shipwreck—foraging for food, building shelter, and sustaining spirits. As leader of this group, Captain Musgrave provides encouragement, requiring times of relaxation as needed. He seems, as a leader, to appreciate when to lean in with guidance and when to cheer initiative. For 18-months, Captain Musgrave and his group withstood the isolation and deprivation through adaptation, ingenuity, and cooperative efforts.

A larger group of castaways, who were shipwrecked four months after Musgrave's group, fared much less well. Their tale, as one reviewer remarked, was in some ways like an adult version of *Lord of the Flies*. From their shipwreck at the foot of cliffs through later events, this group's lethargic treks and decisions too late or not at all accumulate failure after failure in taking the actions needed for survival. With the low energy and inflexibility of this second group and its official leader, you can broadly predict why their tale would be so different—with just one seaman having the resourcefulness needed to face such dire circumstances.

The detail of the narration is engaging. The book also describes norms of master-servant relations of the time, notes the behaviors of government officials, and chronicles some subsequent history of this "graveyard for ships." Lessons emerge naturally from the recreation of a distant time, in a far-away place, through deftly reimagined conversations and events that are freshly relevant today. When the world waits and watches from elsewhere, tales of survival offer possibility for hope. But they also highlight the limits to being able to survive alone.

March 21, 2022

Angel to Grifter to…??

Archangel Michael defeats Satan
by Guido Reni (1575-1642) Santa Maria della Concerzione.
This image is in the Public Domain {{PD-US-expired}}
https://commons.wikimedia.org/wiki/File:GuidoReni_MichaelDefeatsSatan.jpg

In 1952, the iconic educator Robert Maynard Hutchins completed publication of the substantial, multi-volume *Great Books of the Western World.* These include two volumes discussing a hundred or so *Great Ideas,* as well as detailing references to these ideas in the Great Books. This has special interest as the United States continues to travel its extended exposé of the white-ants of democracy–and, who knows, perhaps their eventual accountability?

Reading now what Hutchins and his editors compiled seven decades ago offers some insight about the values in prominence then, compared to the present. The complete *Great Books* was exploratory and ambitious in many ways, but it inevitably incorporated some assumptions of that time that are not acceptable today, including sexist language and the conscious exclusion of Eastern thought.

Importantly though, and more positively, the *Great Ideas* that are discussed in Volumes I and II, along with the entire 54 volumes, illuminate many personal values considered important to daily life–like **wisdom, courage, temperance,** and **justice**. Unsurprisingly, not so extolled are the modern media's five main preoccupations of "Disaster, Celebrity, Crime, Sex, and Violence."

The *Great Ideas* commence with "Angel," then continue alphabetically through "Good and Bad," "Government" and so on, to eventually wrap up with "World." "Grifters" don't rate a mention, although we know from other sources that, along with "Charlatans" and "Crooks," these certainly found their way into all sorts of places, including government then and now.

As early as the "Cs" the trend is clear, as "Citizen" is given its due, along with "Constitution, Courage, Custom and Convention." Publishing so soon after the world's narrow escape from the domination of notorious tyrants in Europe and Asia, Hutchins and his editors also thought "Democracy, Dialectic, and Education" were each worth individual attention.

Further along alphabetically, "Happiness" is priority enough to capture 26 pages of exploration (pp. 684-710). The separate treatments of "Law" and "Liberty" collect 50 pages more–before "Life and Death," "Logic," and "Love" take 67 pages–to close out the first of two volumes on what *Great Ideas* mattered to civilization. You get the idea, so to speak.

The second volume also has interesting reminders on perspective, including "Oligarchy, Principle, and Punishment," before explaining the values in "Reasoning, Rhetoric, and Sense," or contrastingly in "Sin and Slavery." Maybe it's not entirely coincidence that "Truth" and "Tyranny" are alphabetical neighbors, while described together are "Virtue and Vice," as well as "War and Peace."

It was something of a relief to reach, at *Great Idea* number 101, a 16-page exploration of "Wisdom," before concluding the volumes with an ambitious explanation of "World." Much here that is clarifying. For example, whether for past or present concerns, in a nod to wisdom, many of us will agree with Aquinas that "Free choice is part of...dignity."

June 28, 2022

Rip Van Who?

Rip Van Winkle
by John Quidor (1801-1881), Art Institute of Chicago.
This image is in the Public Domain {{PD-US-expired}}
https://en.wikipedia.org/wiki/Rip_Van_Winkle#/media/File:Depiction_of_Rip_Van_Winkle_by_John_Quidor_(1829).jpg

Do you sometimes wish you'd fallen into a long sleep early in 2020 like the fabled Rip Van Winkle? Look around and you will find some people did.

When you encounter anyone like Rip, it's best to be careful. Rip didn't understand much when he met the silent ghosts of Henry Hudson's crew, playing a game of nine-pins in the Catskill Mountains. He didn't ask who they were, or how they knew his name. He did get their magic purple liquor when he imbibed it, putting him to sleep. It worked well for him to miss the American Revolutionary War.

So, chances are that if you're on an evening or early morning walk trying to social distance from the joggers and dog-walkers, or wherever, when you find someone sleeping or sleepwalking through the twenty-first century, this person won't get much about the present reality either.

There are people to shake awake still. Ever since memory, the USA has yet to turn out the higher percentages of voters recorded in some countries. Getting out the vote, person-to-person, door-to-door is the powerful method to do this, with facemasks on (not just by phone or the even weaker ways of other social media).

Meantime, to out-think and out-do the propagandist, George Orwell (1946), Vance Packard (1957), Jacques Ellul (1962), and a host of others have provided us with ways to deal with the continuous propaganda that often numbs the "sleepers," and all of us.

For example, Jacques Ellul named the counteractions you can take against a continuous propaganda onslaught.

1. Challenge any propaganda targeting our pre-existing attitudes AND reassert our beliefs in **honesty, justice, temperance, courage,** and **wisdom**—and our desire to live in a society that enables **health, jobs, shelter, food, safety, freedom,** with any bad actor held **accountable.**

2. Highlight the harm to people by those using anti-democratic actions to deny **health care, jobs, safety, postal services,** etc. AND say exactly what should happen instead.

3. Reassert the rightness of **facts**, positively and specifically (without naming the lie or the liar, to avoid being a megaphone for the corrupt).

4. Keep repeating what is **right** (propaganda decays over time, especially when crowded out of the public communication channels).

Oh, and as George Orwell urged about any verbal refuse, be sure to call out and **mock the foreign propaganda** that misses our culture. As we saw in another blog posting, titled "Going High," this is very easy when it's half-baked with lots of "tells."

Too many of our fellow "we, the people" might seem to be awake in their sleep-walk, as they continue to be polite about a propagandist. But some have taken years to publicly call a lie a lie. And some in the media still broadcast unfiltered drivel of a propagandist; or, endlessly micro-analyze this nonsense, thereby promoting the propagandist and the nonsense. Maybe they have some dangerously mistaken belief that this serves some purpose of even-handedness, or democratic debate, or advertising sales.

I even heard a federal senator this week say, completely unacceptably, that the shame for the failure of his opponents to act properly was on his opponents. How about what that senator had not accomplished holding them to account? He wasn't elected to be a bystander.

During this *Big Sleep*, with apologies to Raymond Chandler, many **"we, the people"** patiently expected someone else to stop the useless growth of lawyers taking legal actions. Providing employment for lawyers wasn't supposed to be a main outcome of democracy. Yet too many such proceedings continue in multiple, drawn-out, inconclusive actions, instead of anything useful to stop the propagandist.

Lookalike despots, autocrats, and wannabe leaders flourish when they are unchecked. There's still time to block and check in workable ways.

One step we can all help with NOW is to personally encourage friends, family, and neighbors to get out the vote.

September 29, 2020

Change or Be Changed

Gulliver Taking His Final Leave of the Land of the Houyhnhnms
by Sawrey Gilpin (1733-1807), Yale Center for British Art. This image is in the Public Domain {{PD-US-expired}} https://commons.wikimedia.org/wiki/File:Gulliver-taking-his-final-leave-of-the-land-of-the-houyhnhnms-sawrey-gilpin.jpg

Gulliver's visit to the Land of the Houyhnhnms, at one level is an engaging exploration of values, scrutinizing the good and bad sides of reason versus emotions. Perhaps horse-lovers feel comforted focusing on the nobility of the calm and rational Houyhnhnms versus the wild Yahoos.

Without delving here into the layers of Jonathan Swift's satire, this episode of fiction certainly raises concerns that matter right now. For sure, re-reading Swift is recommended.

As we chart the future, we probably need little reminding that today's juggernaut of inappropriate framing of much public communication does not serve us well. With the endless news cycle, added to social media and other community gossip, the communication landscape continues to grow more challenging—especially with the continuous fog of the not-really-latest "breaking news."

Yet, with the ever-widening gap between the theory and reality of any Hatch Act enforcement to keep public officials accountable, this is no time to be faint-hearted, inattentive, or distracted.

It's truly unfortunate to recall that in my first blog, little more than three months ago, I suggested that "after some trial fits and starts... much education at all levels might be mainly online–maybe for a long time." With children and teens in many places returning to school over recent weeks, we now start to learn that new Covid-19 infections are greatest in children and teens in some areas.

Although much is being done by many, in efforts to protect and treat people, much more change and inventiveness will be needed going forward. It looks like everyone who cares will have to keep alert to how to remedy the effects of Yahoo behaviors.

August 31, 2020

Whose Challenge?

Young Girl with Fish Bowl
by Mabel May Woodward, Shannon's Fine Art Milford, CT
is in the Public Domain {{PD-US-expired}} https://commons.wikimedia.org/wiki/File:
%27Young_Girl_with_Fish_Bowl%27_by_Mabel_May_Woodward.jpg

Often barely noticeable, like the passing of the date on the calendar for the change of seasons last week, are many adjustments to how we live. No such luck with the impact of Covid. This was clear early. Unfortunately, the projections in my first blog post in May last year of likely changes in services for daily needs, education, and other areas of life were close to what happened. It seems crystal-ball gazing can get some things right.

From the 1970s, Heidi and Alvin Toffler scrutinized data to make large-scale, largely accurate predictions about the world we now live in. They were also mostly right about many details. From the same time, I recall predictions that we'd pay about the same price for water in a bottle as for wine, and people would be talking on portable communicators everywhere—suggestions that were considered unlikely. Yet, despite my years of eye-opening experience of people in politics and the media, still unanticipated was the sheer craven behavior of some wannabe leaders, who were elected to be responsible firstly for the safety and health of all of us. Who, other than the craven or complete cynics, would predict the ramshackle response of these individuals to the pandemic in the United States?

For all the ongoing efforts of countless healthcare workers and so many other service providers, whom we literally applauded in symbolic and substantive statements of support last year, here we are. With many regions well-vaccinated, and others not, and with continuing threats to the supply chain for household goods and other key imports—thanks to the backlog of ships awaiting entry to the wharves of major ports.

Part of this challenge is the ongoing threat of the anti-vax, anti-mask self-proclaimed elite, determined to endanger themselves and everyone else. A larger challenge is leadership that's lackluster or worse in too many places, hampering recovery efforts. We all know that this affects everyone. Even a child who cares for goldfish soon learns that murky water in the fishbowl is everyone's challenge.

One lesson hopefully learned during the last five years in the United States is that the self-deluded, right along with the grifters and charlatans, will keep thriving on distortions, unless each of us makes the effort to dismantle their oppositions to reality. When will there ever be enough pressure on the social media companies, elected officials, charlatans, and some heads of foreign governments, who dangerously white-ant our safety and health with well-publicized nonsense? What's very clear by now is what doesn't work: NEITHER the half-baked approach called "fact-checking," NOR repeating a propagandist's "messages" in the negative!

Getting the attention of anyone to change behavior requires smart use of the motivation process. How to encourage change in someone who is opposed to a proposition has been known for a long time. Still useful are the steps John A. McGee shared, for example, in 1929 in his book *Persuasive Speaking,* now out of copyright and freely available on the Internet, with a helpful table in his book, in Appendix C, at pages 268-9. McGee's basic principles remain a good guide for some purposes. Briefly, when seeking to change the actions of people opposed to a proposition, McGee advocated that we:

1. Secure common ground by first emphasizing any agreement in attitudes, beliefs, or experiences–he described how to seek agreement on general principles, to apply a principle to the specific problem.

2. Anticipate and overpower objections with facts and testimony that demonstrate your approach is the best solution; explain it and offer proof that it removes the cause of a shared problem, using testimony that's credible in the eyes of your audience, with examples of successes.

3. Make the results of the solution vivid with imagery, impelling motives and projections for the audience into the future, while being beware of exaggeration.

4. Request definite action, with specific ways that individuals can help, appealing to habit.

If this all sounds too long and logical, take confidence that folks who get creative have found simple, visual, and emotive ways to put a strategy like this into practice for thousands of years. McGee was just one of the first in more recent times to outline the steps so clearly.

Perhaps it's worth trying an alternative to filling the media and the air with conversations that perpetuate the divisiveness of propagandists. Smallpox, tuberculosis, polio, and too many pandemics since were eradicated not only thanks to the brilliant development and delivery of life-saving vaccines.

Equally important was finding ways to enable reality laggards to ***just get over it!***

October 1, 2021

Catnip Curse

Black and white cat
by Rosendahl. This image is in the Public Domain.
https://commons.wikimedia.org/wiki/File:Black_and_white_cat.jpg

Germaine Greer described herself during an Address to the National Press Club of Washington DC, on 18 May 1971, as a "media freak." Her comments were certainly catnip for the media. She was promoting her just released book *The Female Eunuch*. Yes, now about half a century ago.

She urged women to invent new ways to deal with the truly violent man. Rather than learning karate, she pointed out that karate or other rule-based reactions don't work against the genuinely violent.

Greer shrewdly observed that the genuinely violent doesn't muck about with Marquess of Queensberry rules; rather he uses "a broken bottle, a wheel brace, a tire lever or an axe. He does not see the fight through but seeks to end it quickly by doing as much harm as he can as soon as he can," she said.

Any of us observing the genuinely amoral might get the analogy. Whether you are dealing with an amoral person physically or otherwise, it's best to know that the norms of karate or boxing or equivalent conventional rule-based schema don't apply.

When your opponent lacks stability and is obsessed with self-preservation, character flaws function like catnip. You might get opportunity for just one response. And you better hit the right spot so to speak; per another sporting analogy, you better not be counting on a "Hail Mary."

To reframe this as a fable: A cat will lay in wait sometimes for days observing the patterns of one scurrying mouse. Put catnip into the mix and all semblance of rules leave the scene. So maybe it will help to think of your genuinely amoral, not stable opponent as being about as predictable as a big cat on catnip. How will you deal with this, without being able to count on the equivalent of Animal Control?

As Aesop might say: **The true leader is proved by the quality of action.**

November 12, 2020

Speaking & Writing

Why Read? Why Write?

Two boys in Laos laugh over the book "What Can You Do with an Extra Dinosaur?" which one of them received as his first book.
by Blue Plover/Big Brother Mouse is licensed under CCA-SA 3.0 Unported.
https://commons.wikimedia.org/wiki/File:Books_that_make_literacy_fun.jpg

Answers to "why write?" are probably as many as why we read. Whether from the spontaneous response "...because I have to" or answers more thoughtfully explored with authors, such as in the Paris Review Interviews, maybe not everyone will agree reading and writing are acts of thinking.

For example, as *LitHub* noted yesterday, Ray Bradbury put a sign over his typewriter which read "Don't think!" on the principle, he said, that "...you must *feel*. Your intellect is always buried in that feeling anyway." Perhaps the sign helped Mr. Bradbury follow his own imperative; yet he seemed to feel his writing did also involve thinking and just advocated feeling over thinking to avoid a writer's sin of over-thinking.

And, of course, writing from the heart to the heart, even to move the mind, most would acknowledge is good advice. Whether we believe language is driven by thought or thought is driven by language, and whatever the debunkers of "book-learning" might claim, it's a no-brainer that the love of words is clearly important.

Yet, as reader or writer, consciously and/or unconsciously, I believe that we think... yes, even when we're lost in the escapist fun of worlds that words create. Had Darwin attended to readers and writers as groups to classify, maybe he'd have seen this as a common basis for bundling "readers-writers" together as one group, or at least close to each other. Certainly, any writer is also a reader.

As children growing up, we might not get the significance of parents who encourage reading: the parent who reads a story or more every day or every night to a young child; the related behavior of giving books to one another in the family; and a parent's habit of just reading the news every morning, while not burning the breakfast toast. All are activities that influence how growing children come to think about a life that includes reading and writing.

I've yet to hear any decent case to deny, on the weekend, a child's habit of weekday reading at home after school—even if it means, in the late weekend-afternoon, disappearing from playmates or a family gathering for a while. The worlds of words explored, for many children, we know will help shape occupational success. Importantly too, when this habit is enjoyed, it can help kids in lots of ways, setting a foundation that's passed forward.

When teaching writing with my former colleague Roslyn Petelin years ago, we were always surprised and more than a little dismayed that so many of our very bright first-year university students were starting a communication degree program but could not write very well. Soon enough we redesigned the first-week's writing class to provide just a few introductory remarks, followed by a grammar test that also specifically sought thoughts about writing. Year after year, what the students' test responses told us, both by their poor knowledge of grammar and by their shared thoughts about writing, was that while most wanted to write well their school experience had not adequately prepared them. Students had serious gaps in basic knowledge of conventional language use. Even knowledge of spelling, punctuation, or grammar was lacking.

In their earlier schooling, high-flowered "creativity" or plagiarism seemed then to be most often rewarded. Of course, as Roslyn and I acknowledged when sharing these issues at a National Reading Association conference, some students forget or didn't pay attention when language lessons appeared in their schooling, but the scale of students' ignorance and antagonism about writing was massive. This was especially so from the 1960s through the 1990s, in many countries. Importantly, the responses to the diagnostic test we administered also detailed the individual needs to address.

Using principles for teaching reader-based prose, we set clear steps for students to be able to communicate genuinely with people, as steps to write interactively. We focused ways to identify the key issues that concerned readers and applied a problem-solving approach to teach writing, which Linda Flower and others had developed.

In that other time in another country, what was not so evident was one of the greatest values of reading and writing. Today, the free inquiry that fuels reading and writing becomes even more pertinent as a re-run of McCarthyist-like outrage seeks to dominate the media and our lives in the United States. And, in any other countries where look-alike populist propagandists also twist words and thinking, seeking to undermine democracy.

While acknowledging the critical need for civics education and action, at least equally important is the very developed ability to think clearly, which comes from reading and writing. As Isocrates noted, "We regard speaking well to be the clearest sign of a good mind, which it requires; and truthful, lawful, and just speech we consider the image of a good and faithful soul." Unless deeply into incantations or some propagandist's stimuli, we can feel secure that reading, writing, and simple dialogue will nurture free thought, which is how propaganda dies.

May 31, 2021

What We Say

Audrey Hepburn for My Fair Lady
by movie studio, publicity photo. This image is in the Public Domain.
https://commons.wikimedia.org/wiki/File:Audrey_Hepburn_-_1964.jpg

Way back when, Australian schoolchildren would challenge each other to spell what we understood was the scientific name for that unusual mammal, the Platypus.

By school-age, Aussie kids had sidestepped hazards beyond the schoolyard, surviving some of the world's most deadly jellyfish, sharks, snakes, spiders, and more. So, faced with the local version of a schoolkid jibe that somehow flew around the world before the Internet, the smart kids would reply to the daunting challenge of **"Ornithorhynchus is a hard word, spell it,"** by simply answering, **"I...T,"** choosing to focus on the literal meaning of the sentence.

For anyone with an interest in words though, what words suggest, rather than what they denote, might hold special interest. Pioneering professors of phonetics showed how we say more than what we literally mean in our choice of words. It was the character, Professor Henry Higgins, in George Bernard Shaw's play *Pygmalion* and Higgins's subsequent appearance in the Rodgers and Hammerstein musical version, *My Fair Lady*, that popularized some wide awareness of how language choice and pronunciation marked class stratification. The character of Higgins was based in part on the pioneering, prolific but cantankerous British professor of phonetics, Henry Sweet.

Beyond this, the words we choose tell much about us, as later linguists and psychologists have shown. They know more than we do ourselves about the meanings we share, through the words we choose and how we speak.

For example, in the early twentieth century, European researchers speculated that a high ratio of nouns (and their related adjectives, articles etc.) to verbs (and their related adverbs etc.) might be a flag for people having some psychological challenges. Linguistic researchers have long noted that someone using many verbs versus nouns projected a more in-touch, vigorous personality. Ongoing research has refined clues about noun/verb ratios and other language features, to help diagnose and treat some serious psychological conditions. In more recent decades, the computerized counting of word types, along with content analyses, have helped to extend the understanding of some effects from a variety of the accumulated language features.

We can all recognize the sleep-inducing effect of bureaucratic messages, with complex sentences and too much passive voice or past tense verbs. And, breaking an old grammatical "rule," what about the very great value of using the little word "and" to begin a sentence, or just more frequently–and connect thoughts, as we do in conversation. Jonathan Swift and some other powerful writers used "and" a lot, which helped to keep us interested in what they had to say, by making them seem more conversational. So, the revelations abound–when you realize what to look for.

Even a small variation from an expected style might have big effects. It was the researcher Mr. E.H. Flint, in the early 1970s, who pointed out to our class that sentence fragments (a.k.a. non-principal sentences, to the traditional grammarian) uniquely occurred in the spoken language and not the samples of written Australian English that he was reviewing at the time.

The big deal he pointed out to us was how dramatically even a single sentence fragment in writing helped to create an informal, conversational effect. That President Biden used 38 sentence fragments in his Inaugural Address, as I noted in another blog post, had a really big effect. I wonder what Mr. Flint would have thought of the eminent British linguist, David Crystal's publishing a book with the title *Txting: The gr8 db8*, as long ago as 2008; much less the ongoing shifts in what we now consider formal or colloquial or intimate language.

Beyond the strengths found in how language choices influence what we think about the tone and style of a speaker or writer, there are even more enjoyments in these Elysian Fields–for example, looking at how word choice, sentence form, and passage construction "Xtra-verbally" influence the potency of emotional appeals, or the effectiveness of an argument, or other communication effects.

A field far from the Elysian Fields also contains the bad folks who continuously deny, distract, or delay, by putting the small word "not" in front, to say they are not advocating something or other, when they really are. In relation to so-called "fact-checking," like most car drivers who genuinely don't see cyclists, we don't see the NOT and focus again on the lie; and when we repeat a statement from these folks, with "not" upfront, we're really helping to state what they said, the lie, again and again and again.

Then, to come right up to date, there's a whole other field of positive-sounding words like "Remember this day forever;" which, given the context, is quite the hyperbolic signal to strengthen commitment to nasty actions that I believe even schoolkids might know are NOT democratic.

Once we more consciously look at the meanings of words well beyond the "thing" or concept that a word represents, it's kind of like wearing X-ray glasses from science fiction—you might want to keep your vision adjusted and never want to take your new X-ray glasses off.

February 10, 2021

What the Inaugural Address Means

"We Hold These Truths" at Jefferson Memorial
by Billy Hathorn. This image is licensed under CCA-BY-3.0 Unported.
https://commons.wikimedia.org/wiki/File:%22We_Hold_These_Truths%22_
at_Jefferson_Memorial_IMG_4729.JPG

The recent inaugural address of the new president of the United States was distinct in both content and style.

Most important was the outline of policies to reassert truth, law, and justice as national values. Importantly too, the language of the inaugural address signaled a novel integration of analytical and intuitive styles.

I was interested to hear this different language mix from President Biden, having just compared the language of the previous president with ten notable speakers from the 1890s to 1980. Compared with these speakers, the outgoing president had the most intuitive communication style.

In contrast, President Biden blended a mix of content and function words that reinstated an analytical communication style in the presidency, while also incorporating some language features that suggested an intuitive approach.

The speech was structured to logically address problems facing the nation and to offer solutions. Language features included a substantial number of complete sentences, low occurrences of non-referential adverbs, prepositions, and impersonal pronouns, as well as a strong presence of such common rhetorical devices as *anaphora* and other parallelism, *antitheses,* and other features that reinforced a conceptual, analytical communication style. It also derives some punch from a frequency of verbs and verbals, especially action verbs, infinitives, and participles.

The speech was delivered in a largely conversational tone. This combined with accumulations of many very short sentences, 38 sentence fragments, quite a few occurrences of "we/our" and imperatives, some questions, use of "and" to begin sentences and phrases, interpolations, and relatively few conjunctions, all helping to suggest an intuitive approach.

Why this matters is that, as mentioned in another blog post, a study published by the *National Academy of Sciences* not long ago had noted a decline of the analytical communication style in American presidents and other English-speaking political leaders since about 1980. Apparently "voters are increasingly drawn to leaders who can make difficult, complex problems easier to understand with intuitive, confident answers."

Since the later twentieth century, mostly gone from popular taste are the long, grand rhetorical flourishes, replaced first by the conversational language and tones required on radio and television, then more recently by a snappy resonance demanded in social media.

After the perversions of brief and snappy into untruthful, illegal, and unjust, to deliver whatever is most outrageous, perhaps we are to see whether outrageous language might more often get shunted aside by a quieter rhetoric in an analytical communication style—which is buttressed with an intuitive approach.

Perhaps it's not a total pipe dream to hope that the mix of content words in the inaugural address that refers to people, tangible things, and real concepts might open the way for further, similar public communications that reference reality.

Can we even hope these continue to get some media attention, instead of the covey of "audience-tested" outrage words delivered into talking points and media releases that have become so common for too long?

January 22, 2021

Surf

Kawana, Australia
by Finnrussell99 is licensed under CCA-SA-4.0 International.
https://commons.wikimedia.org/wiki/File:Kawana,_Australia.jpg

New Year for a couple of decades marked the final stage of three-weeks at the beach when growing up. Apart from a few seasonal celebrations, visits with relatives or friends, and some movies, this annual vacation was a time of uninterrupted surfing, of both waves and words.

Early every morning in a land of endless summer, the family carried beach umbrella, rolled-up beach mat, towels, boogie boards, sunglasses, sunscreen, drink-containers, and of course books, to trek in caravan formation across sand-hills and the already hot beach sand—to find just the right spot, between the flags placed by the lifesavers to mark the area safe for swimming.

The morning was spent in the surf—after a quick survey of what the previous night's tides and weather had set as the surfing terrain, to make safe navigation across any deep gutters, rip-currents, or sandbars—out far, to where serious waves gathered—there to catch a deeply rolling swell the long distance to shore, riding on its final curl and roll onward to the beach.

Swimming with the swell to catch a wave more than two-to-three-times one's height was learned early, for an exhilarating ride as close as you'd hope to the beach. Sometimes, misjudged timing delivered an additional lesson as a human cork, tumbling in the wave or hitting the sand hard, with eyes wide open underwater, shrouded with flurries of white bubbles and sand clouds, until breaking the surface for air. Eventually we'd come back to the beach umbrella and outspread towels, talking and reading, until returning home for lunch.

During the long hot afternoons, in separate places–indoors, under trees, or in the sand-hills, lots of reading revealed more than the year's schooling about how words work. Being carried along by words for the afternoon was different but, in some ways, similar to the morning's experience riding the waves.

Even from everyday Aussie talk, we were well primed to be curious about exploring language, often encountering analogy, rhyming substitutions, abbreviation, imaginative omission, and lots of figurative language. Not everywhere in the world will you hear the phrase "like a lizard drinking" with everyone around you understanding this translates to "busy"–because a lizard lies "flat out" busily drinking at the billabong… and it's commonly known that a billabong is a particular type of watering hole and not a surfing reference, despite the confusion created by this now also being a popular brand-name for surfing gear and clothing.

Or how many people do you know who, out of the blue, refer to a best friend and/or spouse as "china plate," or just "china," or "plate"? Of course, Cockneys and Aussies know what this is because there's a rhyme with "mate," and everyone knows what that means, right! These are some of what are better known among quite a large trove of Australian/"Oz-talk"–now, that's "clear as mud" you might say, but will you routinely put these and many more language adaptations and adoptions, one after another continuously in every sentence you speak?

No wonder that John O'Grady, writing under his pseudonym Nino Culotta, sold so many copies of *They're a Weird Mob*–a 1957 comic novel about an Italian immigrant to Oz trying to work all this out. And, then there's Frank Hardy's irreverently humorous satire *The Outcasts of Foolgarah*—which would require too many blog posts to translate from Oz-talk, however imprecisely.

Later, it was kind of surprising to find thoughtful authors, mainly from Europe or North America, who bothered to write entire books about tropes, rhetorical style, slang, or colorful language. Mostly these authors were interested in how words are used differently in different places, or for different purposes. It didn't take long to catch curiosity about how we shape words and words shape us—which also primed curiosity about how a writer like Dylan Thomas opened a path to sounds, sights, and insights (Thomas, 1949, "Poem in October" and "In My Craft or Sullen Art," read by the poet, referenced below). Or, of his venturing outside in winter Quite Early One Morning, describing a seaside Welsh village and its people waking to another day (Thomas, 1944), as he makes intriguing entrances to unfamiliar scenes and feelings, via his unique rhythm, symbols, and density of lyrical language.

Then Charles Darwin describing human origins in language attentive to his wife's deeply different faith, to an eye-opening James Baldwin telling it on the mountain, to "Rabbie" Burns's reshaping songs and stories of Scotland, to Judith Wright visualizing the Australian bush, to Halldór Laxness's vision of independence, to the wit of Wisława Szymborska, and so many other worlds of words.

Along the way, seeds from the thoughtful authors on rhetoric and language style progressively grew further curiosity—so it continues—recently and enjoyably, with much thanks to a friend, who pointed out yet another thoughtful author known on his weblog as *The Inky Fool*. This is Mark Forsyth, who dives into, if you'll allow the metaphor, oceans of words... and, who seems to have way too much fun with explanations of etymology, syntax, semantics, and rhetoric.

For anyone even a little interested in stretching understandings of what words can do, Mr. Forsyth, with an energy worthy of a surfer, dives into allusion, diacope, and other examples of rhetorical style, to explain how certain everyday language in movies or songs, or other word experiences, manage to carry us along.

If this is the nearest that a lexicographer comes in an armchair to surfing waves of words, good luck to us all. You can join in, and hopefully enjoy starting the year with one of his videos…

Happy New Year…

Notes

Dylan Thomas (1944), *Quite Early One Morning,*
    https://www.youtube.com/watch?v=ayhGlv-bceY
Dylan Thomas (1949), Reads "Poem in October" and "In My Craft or Sullen Art,"
    Columbia LP, issued in 1950 on Columbia Masterworks label, catalogue number
    ML4259, https://www.youtube.com/watch?v=3XMaJanGuWI
Mark Forsyth (2020), *What Makes a Movie Line Memorable? Diacope,*
    https://www.youtube.com/watch?v=oo5Ikx3F5ak

January 1, 2022

Violent Rhetoric

The Hon. Peter Lalor MLA, Speaker of the Legislative Assembly of Victoria, 1880-1887
by Ludwig Becker (1808?-1861). This image is in the Public Domain {{PD-US-expired}}
https://commons.wikimedia.org/wiki/File:Peter_Lalor.jpg

Not a new phenomenon. How about from Patrick Henry? "Give me liberty or give me death" (in 1775). Or, from Australia's Peter Lalor at the Eureka stockade? "We swear by the Southern Cross to stand truly by each other and fight to defend our rights and liberties" (in 1854).

Yet, hearing a broadcast anchor object to the "violent rhetoric" of the crowd who worship AR-15's and oversized engines to impose their egos on others still felt new. In all three disputes, what's common are differences that do not allow for solution, other than by winning. Part of what's "new" is that, in the first two cases, visiting terror on others is not threatened. And some of us still believe that violence is supposed to be contained in civilized society.

Norms and Laws

When propagandist self-dealers rule by threatening the safety of the rest of us by sweeping aside norms and laws, all the handwringing in the media will only do so much for a nation's self-correction. Voting might only do so much too.

Pundits still talk as if norms and laws are going to spring back, resuscitated, and freed from the grip of bad actors. IMHO, no laws and certainly no norms by themselves, even assuming they are diligently and actively executed, will truly control the bad actor whose smarts are every minute pursuing crooked actions.

National Self-correction

Some political theorists still claim that oversight committees and whistleblower public servants, who see their professional lives destroyed, provide *"relentless public scrutiny"* and *"transparency."*

Unless national self-correction is backed, as appropriate, with punishment, intervention/therapy or "surgery," then representative democracy faces a rocky road ahead. Of course, joining the AR-15 crowd, who want to copy the most infamous barbarians, before and since Xerxes crossed the Hellespont to conquer Athens back in 480 BC, might be attractive to barbarians.

No sane person wants a repeat of the human history that saw loss of lives in battles on a scale equivalent to what Covid-19's short trajectory has caused already. Mostly, some of us would just like the pitch of public talk tamped down. We'd like the promises of life, liberty and the pursuit of happiness assured.

After all, don't we expect the people we elect to deliver peace of mind? Isn't that why our forebears risked so much to demand better of tyrants?

June 19, 2020

Reach

Henry Ward Beecher cartoon as Gulliver reaching out to the "Liliputian" crowd
Gulliver und die Partei-Liliputaner… Cartoon from Puck
by Bernard Gillam (1856-1896), Los Angeles County Museum of Art.
This image is in the Public Domain {{PD-US-expired}}
https://commons.wikimedia.org/wiki/File:Gulliver_und_die_Partei-
Liliputaner_1885_(Henry_Ward_Beecher).jpg

Engaging an audience takes talent. Whether comedian, TV anchor, journalist, or a speaker or writer for any purpose, how you start sets the stage for all that follows. Especially in the snappy world of social media, the choice of visuals as well as your first words matter.

We know that with distractions just a click away, it's best to get attention to topic, theme, and you, quickly! From the earliest teachers of rhetoric onwards, we've known that audiences look for an introduction, a body, and a conclusion; and the best introduction attracts attention to both the topic and the speaker/writer, as well as directly developing the topic. We connect with anyone who does this well.

Clearly, what you choose to mention among facts, opinions, and ideas, along with the words you chose, how you shape sentences, and how you develop passages, all impact how an audience sees you, thinks of you, relates to you, and hears what you say. The talent of making these choices well grows from thinking to do, from thoughtful "listening," and from practice.

During the introduction, as in any first meeting, a listener or reader intuitively looks for common interests, along with signs of who you are in the words you choose–which signal your tone, role, stance, and personality.

When teaching speechwriting, an exercise that I often used to help reveal how language choices project personal style and *persona* (adopted role) was to ask students to read brief speech excerpts, which didn't identify who the speakers were. The students then described what personality characteristics they detected from the language choices, wrapping up with the inevitable guesses about the identity of each speaker.

In common with much teaching of rhetoric, we also listened to the recorded speeches of a wide variety of powerful speakers, to take note of specific language features that resonated.

The speakers of course included Sir Winston Churchill, whose early experience in journalism showed through, with his initially setting a scene, then dramatically relating events to inspire commitment. Or John F. Kennedy's memorable introduction in his inaugural address, urging observance of "not a victory of party but a celebration of freedom." And Martin Luther King Jr's deeply resonant voice, to commence his sharing of a dream, by marking the occasion of the day's march to Washington DC as "the greatest demonstration of freedom." Each alerted listeners to focus the moment.

Some speakers use questions to begin. Mahatma Gandhi asked what non-cooperation was and why was it important; and Jawaharlal Nehru asked what brought "friends and fellow Asians" together. Each, with straightforward engagement, developed tremendous following. Across a range of Australians, from Dame Enid Lyons, Sir Robert Menzies, John Curtin, Oodgeroo Noonuccal, Gough Whitlam, Germaine Greer, and a host of other community leaders and advocates of social change, a similar variety of approaches for introductory remarks is evident.

Even the less savory provided lessons. Such as the opening to Richard Nixon's 1969 inaugural address, where he acknowledged that "In the orderly transfer of power, we celebrate the unity that keeps us free;" indicating how far down the escalator it's all traveled since. Or the rambling Adolf Hitler in 1938, complaining of "the foreign press [who] inundated the new Reich with a virtual flood of lies and calumnies," which hardly deserved repeating, yet some still like to hear their own echoes of that approach.

On the flipside, the nineteenth century's so-dubbed "most famous man in America," Henry Ward Beecher, so the story goes, one hot summer evening walked into his routinely over-crowded church, and the assembled congregation became aware of his uncharacteristically removing his coat and tie and mopping his head with a large handkerchief. Once in the pulpit, with all eyes fixed in his direction, Beecher reportedly exclaimed "It's so goddamn hot in here tonight!" After a pause, he stated that this was what he'd heard someone say as he'd walked into the church; then he delivered a sermon on blasphemy.

Today's audiences might not sit still for the length of sermons and other speeches so common in the nineteenth century. Yet Beecher's introduction stands the test of time, to illustrate how he made full use of the situation and his own movement, combined with careful timing and a very few words, to commence his remarks powerfully.

Choosing well the ideas, nonverbal opportunity, and words we use makes a real difference.

June 30, 2021

Much in Verbs

Much Ado about Nothing by William Shakespeare
by Alfred W. Elmore 1846. This image is in the Public Domain {{PD-US-expired}}
https://commons.wikimedia.org/wiki/File:Much_Ado_About_Nothing_by_Alfred_Elmore_1846.jpg

Shakespeare's play *Much Ado about Nothing* lightly explores human realities and impressions, delivering insights or delights about both. A good deal of repartee or turn-taking among characters in the play relies on verbs or verbal functions, to trigger the nuggets of humor or some wisdom—with quotable quotes like **"...*wooing, wedding* and *repenting is* as a Scotch jig."**

And this play is only one of the many places in literature, in history, and in life that the functions of verbs matter more than we might first notice. Verbs do much beyond what they denote.

From ancient to contemporary history, barbarians have peppered their propaganda with action verbs, seeking to be remembered as "Great," despite bloodthirsty conquests. In 480 BC Xerxes boasted in a tone too recently echoed, "My intent is to ***throw*** a bridge over the Hellespont and ***march*** an army through Europe against Greece, that thereby I ***may obtain*** vengeance..."

Regardless, history recorded a very large difference between the promise and performance, after Xerxes assembled his reportedly huge army and failed to conquer Greece. The famous historian, Herodotus, seems to consider Xerxes a superstitious and bloodthirsty fool. Just behind the veil of "greatness" that tyrants seek are the very real atrocities that their propaganda works to erase, with lies buttressed by strong-sounding language.

Any public communication is worth examining for how verbs energize and/or divert us. Unsurprisingly, news headlines across the world during the last 24 hours deliver mainly action verbs–***casts*** doubt (UK), ***grinds*** on (USA), ***pushes*** back (USA), deficits ***left*** open (Australia), grid emissions ***set to skyrocket*** (Canada), economist ***warns*** (Germany), ***limit*** even more (Mexico), four Jokowi ministers ***may run*** (Indonesia), ***appears to be*** in no rush (France), ***secure*** three seats (Ireland), "…we ***will win…***" (Ukraine), ***takes hit…*** in elections (Netherlands), ***…to establish*** new reception centers (Finland), tax reduction ***eaten up*** (Norway), ***can benefit*** when defence ***has become*** more important (Sweden), ***…makes*** claim (Russia), ***continues*** search (Japan), ***ramps up*** provocations in run-up (South Korea), …and ***expands*** Covid-19 testing (China). The French newspaper headline seems more cognitive, yet the headline writer infers an expectation of more immediate action.

And action verbs matter in more places than just news headlines. The campaign slogans that the advertising industry touts as its most effective variously rely on verbs, adverbs, or (in one case here) a noun that denotes an action. These include within "wha***ss***up" a colloquial ***"ss"*** for "***is*** or ***'s***," the adverbial "always," and the noun "search," suggesting verb functions–…***do***…, …***share***…, …wha***ss***up…, …***tastes*** great…, …always…, …***think*** small…, …in search…, …***got*** milk…, ….***get*** a…, ***Does*** she…, …***is*** forever…, …***smell*** like…, Where***'s*** the beef…, …***thank*** you mom.

Likewise, we can all think of extraordinary speeches that use carefully chosen verbs to stimulate action or new ways of thinking, helping to propel special power in delivery that's long remembered–you ***cannot locate*** it and you ***cannot stop*** it (Emmeline Pankhurst), I ***have*** a dream (Martin Luther King Jr), ***let*** tyrants ***fear*** (HRH Elizabeth I), ***give*** me blood and I ***will give*** you freedom (Subhas Chandra Bose), ***give*** me liberty or ***give*** me death (Patrick Henry), ***ask*** not what America ***will do*** for you, but what together ***we can do*** for the world (John F. Kennedy), the land ***is*** our mother (Oodgeroo Noonuccal), we ***will*** not ***be quiet,*** we ***will*** not ***be controlled*** (Gloria Steinem), we ***have*** nothing ***to fear*** but fear itself (Franklin D. Roosevelt), we ***shall fight*** on the beaches (Sir Winston Churchill), the advertisements ***are*** for women (Germaine Greer), or this subtle use of the verb "to be," …as ***is*** a tale, so ***is*** life: not how long it ***is,*** but how good it ***is, is*** what ***matters*** (Seneca).

We know verbs can help keep language lively and tell us much about the beliefs of a speaker or writer, including the stance on a subject, or any perception of us, the listeners or readers. Worth a look also is the ratio of "verbals" (verbs and their derivatives, like adverbs etc.) to "nounals" (nouns and their derivatives, like adjectives etc.), as well as the occurrences of the verb "to be," or verb pairs, or the infinitive, or the present tense versus other tenses, or passive voice, or the imperative verb—to name just some of the entrances to explore how verbs work.

And verbs provide just one area of language to explore more closely, before venturing further into an Aladdin's cave of the interesting ways of language—such as how function words, rather than content words, reflect thought and attention patterns, from which listeners and readers infer personal qualities, relationships, and types of formality or informality.

A good entry to navigating language effectiveness though is to explore how verbs do more work for us than we might always consider.

May 9, 2022

A Few Words

"The Remarkables" New Zealand, Queenstown 1
by Bernard Spragg NZ is licensed under CC0 1.0 Universal Public Domain Dedication.
https://commons.wikimedia.org/wiki/File:Queenstown_1_(8168013172).jpg

Regularly counted on but little noticed are some words that appear to have not much meaning, but a lot of use. In English, one of the most innocuous words, *the*, is thought to be the word that we use the most.

We may take the article, *the*, for granted partly because it delivers no meaning by itself. Yet some estimates put it at 5% of every 100 words used. Considering that each of us uses an estimated 20,000 words actively (Schumacher 2020), this means this three-letter word carries quite a load in our communication. The way function words like *the* work are specific to a context, and some languages get along just fine without *the* or an equivalent, or use an affix to a word, or a demonstrative in its place.

When you look at some uses of *the*, it's clear why we like to use it so much. *The* helps us understand what's being referred to. In some contexts, it's used to help quantify or identify, for example, "the slice of pie." It signals something special about "the place," rather than just being "a place." It makes distinction between a lapse of memory any of us might have, which nonetheless causes grief to friends, family, and the person who experience it, and concern that this foretells *the* lapse of memory.

Shakespeare has us ponder which King is referred to in *Hamlet* when the guard utters "'Long live *the* King,' soon followed by the apparition of the ghost: 'Looks it not like *the* King?'" This is discussed in a piece from the BBC listed in the bibliography, which points out that *the* serves in this case as "a kind of 'hook'... [used] ...to make us quizzical, a bit uneasy even." As the author of that discussion points out, *the* also adds substance to a phrase like "*the* man in the Moon," with the naming presuming that "he" exists (Jackson).

In this direction, we sometimes use *the* to dignify or attribute power and authority, as in *the* President, but omitting *the* might have different effects in different nations. The British say simply, "Yes, Prime Minister," both for directly addressing the Prime Minister and the for the celebrated television series of that name. On the other hand, people in the United States preface addressing "*the*" President with "Mr.," or in the future "Madam."

In other situations, we use *the* to give concepts gravitas, as in "the climate crisis" or "the silent spring," whether or not all details are known or knowable. In relation to interpreting the United States Constitution, the media and popular usage have probably unwittingly dignified a crop of Associate Justices within the nation's Supreme Court by referring to them as "the originalists."

But *the*, like all words, needs to be understood in the linguistic and broader social context, and "*the* Founders" surely have more dignity, significance, and authority than the so-called "originalists." Both those "originalists" and others pay lip-service, at the very least, to the historical significance and greater wisdom of "*the* Founders." It must therefore be willful blindness of the current propagators of originalism that enables them to conveniently overlook the recorded suggestions from "*the* Founders" that the Constitution would need to be interpreted, adjusted, or changed to accommodate unforeseen or unforeseeable circumstances.

Associate Justice Scalia was politely but firmly invited to explore this broader view as long ago as 2010 when he visited Australia—by Justice Michael Kirby, formerly of the High Court of Australia. I mention this in my book on the persuasive language or notable Australians, in the chapter on Kirby, at pp.181-2. This is available at his website and Kirby's complete "public conversation" with Scalia is noted in the bibliography.

Another word much used in some public talk is *very*. It's used to provide emphasis or assert significance. Pseudo-populists especially overuse *very*—probably because they're attracted to its emphasis of the extreme, without referencing anything specific. They seem to hope that accumulated uses of *very* will make what they're talking about have greater importance than what's merited.

More favored by some public figures is *remarkably*. This seems to resonate with significance or substance in ways that *very* does not. The versatility of *remarkable* and its variants is as the word itself denotes—as long as it's not overused or used in ways that make the person using it seem "stuffy."

At its root meaning, "*remark...*" reminds of situations that involve people, in a way that *very* does not. When we talk about making *remarks*, rather than "speaking" or "presenting" to people, for example, we infer more of a conversational experience. Other nuance, like some sense of scale, is wrapped into *remarkably*, which the vagueness of *very* lacks.

The conservative Australian politician, Sir Robert Menzies, drew on the nuances of *remarkable* and its variants with his *remarkable* speaking ability—engaging audiences and enabling him to retain the role of prime minister for almost 20 years. Against the fears that he stoked about the disunity of his opponents, he recommended the progress accomplished through the stability of his own governments by pointing out to voters that "we have enjoyed in Australia 12 years of *remarkable* growth and *remarkable* prosperity, with a *remarkably* high level of employment, notwithstanding small occasions..."

Likewise, *remarkable* was favored by some Labor prime ministers who were noted for making more substantive commentary, like Gough Whitlam speaking to the Washington Press Club, "In the wake of the *remarkable* events in Indo-China..." or Paul Keating in his Redfern Park Speech, "...we can build a prosperous and *remarkably* harmonious multicultural society..." Also, Justice Michael Kirby, in his law reform advocacy, uses the word for emphasis, "...bring home to us all the *remarkable* changes in the makeup of our country."

And once alerted to the strength of *remarkable*, it seems like the word pops up in many places–rather like the owners of the Volkswagen "Beetle" would notice that Volkswagens were everywhere. It looks like I've caught the habit, at least in the book mentioned earlier, of using *remarkable* and its variants 13 times, in addition to quoting others.

But it's challenging to find a greater visualization of the power of such words than the New Zealanders' name for the mountain range featured in the opening photo to this blog post. Geologists will point out that geologically older mountains are weathered and worn down over time. It's believed Britain's highest peak, Ben Nevis, only survived erosion because it collapsed into a chamber of molten granite magma.

New Zealand's tallest mountain, Aoraki/Mt. Cook, is more than 2.7 times higher than Ben Nevis, being among the many mountains thrust up through New Zealand's "newer" geological activity. Of the words discussed here, it only takes two to spotlight the grandeur and scale of the mountain range neatly and truly as *The Remarkables*.

July 15, 2022

The -ism Family

9-11 Memorial, New York
by Bryan Ledgard is licensed under CCA 2.0 Generic.
https://commons.wikimedia.org/wiki/File:9-11_Memorial,_New_York_(18262804895).jpg

Large, or even dangerously dominant, in people's minds and hearts is a family of words in English with the suffix -ism.

We can all too quickly think of some branch or other of the -ism family tree. The favorites of the 20th century were the feuding cousins, "Fascism" and "Communism." Persistently adversarial also are "Conservatism" and "Liberalism" and "Radicalism" and "Anarchism," seeking the attention of potential devotees. And, on the left or the right, the often noisy claims of "Libertarianism" might pop up, sometimes with the implied question, "what about me?" Or, the calls of "Environmentalism" that ask the question, "what about all of us?"

Then there are the regrettably ever enduring and insidious presumptions of "Racism" and "Sexism." They manage to keep finding followers among legislators, judges, employers, teachers, and parents, as well as some devotees of "Professionalism," or everyday individuals, all of whom keep blighting lives through the centuries.

There's also "Cannibalism" or the arguably, analogically unrelated "Authoritarianism," or "Corporatism," or "Nationalism," or "Nazism," or "Tribalism," or "Populism" or "Cronyism" or "Denialism." Do we need to pay more attention to asking which of these branches in the -ism family are intertwined, or true, or phony? And where are we with "Modernism," or "Postmodernism," or "Relativism"? To mix metaphors some, this is just the tip of the -ism iceberg. The complexity and scale of the -ism family appear substantial.

Of course, "Individualism" is a shining light surely, perhaps the 21st century's most notable champion of -isms? It's easy to add to the catalog of the family members, and we need to exercise care about whether to include some in the family, such as "Opportunism," observed of course only in others.

Then there are the frequent fellow travelers of "Cultism," "Fundamentalism," "Evangelism," and "Originalism." Which might additionally stimulate questions about what happened to "Realism?" So often not welcome in the -ism family. Thanks to the creativity that language permits, we can be swamped with "Neologisms" seeking inclusion in the -ism family. This can be fine, even enjoyable, for anyone with interest in words.

Much trouble comes though when blind devotion to an -ism fuels the underpinning ideology that ignites emotions like greed and hate and fear. Deep-seated greed, hate, and fear drive nasty behavior. And, neither greed nor hate nor fear need look very far for family feuds to copy, like the generations of Hatfields and McCoys, or the Campbells and McDonalds, and who can forget the "joys" of the Montagues and Capulets? When blind devotion is a tinder box, "Extremism" makes commonsense not so common.

With a history of misfortune and tragedy draped over so many -isms, it's reasonable to wonder what will ever slow the propagation and proliferated impact of the -ism family? Mostly, -isms don't comply with control, especially self-control. However much civil society attempts avoidance, containment, or elimination of -isms, these labels, libels, and lip-service to thinking will often just keep on keeping on.

Look at the conveniently recurring use of "Socialism," blathered about in efforts to make outcasts of people from the left, the right, and the center. Then there are "Nudism" and "Idealism," which sound suspiciously similar; best make outcasts of both, just in case. Of course, there's always difficult-to-deal-with "Hedonism," along with "Behaviorism," and digging deep into the barrel of despair there's the ragbag with estranged relatives, "Sadism" and alter ego, "Masochism."

And no need to create "Joyism" or "Extaticism" just because a favorite word of humanity misses family membership by a letter. Yet anything like these could be welcome to crack the door on some real joy, or everyday peace, or safety at least, from those resurgent expressions of "Elitism," now in the form of the anti-vax, anti-mask devotees who dictate life in this Covid world, with their behavior threatening themselves and everyone else.

Fortunately, the great value of language and its relation to thinking is that the ability of each of us to create our own landscape for living is within each of us. Whether or not we'll ever have command of all the genealogical branches of the -ism family is unclear. Meantime, do you think it would help to think carefully before resorting to -ism talk?

Maybe too, we should listen to George Orwell, who really did know a thing or two about such matters. It's more than time to heed his good advice to **jeer loudly enough to send some of these lumps of verbal refuse into the dustbin where they belong.**

9/11, Never Forget.

September 11, 2021

Style

Penguin in Antarctica jumping out of the water
by Christopher Michel (1967-) is licensed CCA 2.0 Generic.
https://commons.wikimedia.org/wiki/File:Penguin_in_Antarctica_jumping_out_of_the_water.jpg

The popular singer Sting has it. Along with Aretha Franklin, Stevie Wonder, Herbie Hancock, and so many more musical talents in the ten-year retrospective recently celebrating International Jazz Day—they all had it. Then, in very different ways in their glory days, so did Bob Dylan and Shirley Bassey and Mozart and Beethoven, and Jack Benny and David Letterman, oh, and what about Charlie Chaplin and so many more?

In the movie business, so concerned to promote style, even Charlton Heston and John Wayne had it, yet so did Bugs Bunny, Daffy Duck, and Charlie Brown. Of a completely different character, so did Audrey Hepburn or Grace Kelly. Long ago, in the full-blown age of Hollywood invention was the "It-girl," Clara Bow, who became a role model, says the Smithsonian, for women who were free of the domestic sphere.

Also, for earlier generations, Ingrid Bergman, Ginger Rogers and Fred Astaire had style, yet so did Groucho Marx, together with other famous and everyday folks. All with some distinction from each other, and sometimes with commonalities, to make the composite we call style.

Some people so want style, perhaps thinking their world will be so much better... that maybe fame or treasure will follow, if they attain IT. Yet Greta Thunberg and Amanda Gorman clearly have a different depth and purpose in their styles, as does Glenda Jackson. Then, there are various worlds of style in the arts, literature, and public life.

For many, style is bound within a job or role, like speechwriters who daily seek style in words, and even in her days of grief, Queen Elizabeth has it. Is style the person?

Related hard-to-answer questions persist—Is style distinct from content? Or are these convenient descriptors one? Are there good and bad styles? Does the tabloid press have style, or a style? Do the cringeworthy who creep into public life have style? Their followers think so.

What's clear is that *style* means many different things to different people.

One approach for examining style says that whether in language or life, it's about choices. In this view, what we choose in facts, opinions, ideas, or actions, along with the words, sentence shape, and passage development we use is what delivers style.

Fact is we do say a lot to others in the words we choose and what we do, beyond the "message" supposedly denoted in words or actions. Always best to remember that communication happens in the mind of the listener, reader, or observer when interpreting what we express.

To explore how our language projects style, a whole area of study called "stylistics" has produced, over many decades, an eclectic range of approaches to find or assess style, in literature, speeches, the media, professional interactions, daily conversation, comedy, and so on.

In some quite intriguing looks at language, these describers of language style tell much about what words do to suggest conversational or formal tone, personality, family or geographical origins, occupation or profession, disposition toward an audience, and a host of other "tells."

Some discourse analysts even say they can distill systems of belief, a.k.a. ideology, in language style. Can't help wondering how much their own ideological lens determines what they find?

Among the many explanations and explorations of this field of stylistics, one that nicely overviews approaches to literary style is on *Aunty Muriel's blog,* "What is stylistics?" Another overview, pertinent to how we use language to persuade is the detailed text, *Rhetorical Style: The Uses of Language in Persuasion* by Jeanne Fahnestock; also, of course, always worth another look is to catch up on the latest from the eminent British linguist, David Crystal, via his ever-growing website.

Perhaps style is the person... certainly seems so for the many resilient explorers and explainers of language.

May 2, 2021

We or Me?

Social media faces
by Gerd Altmann is licensed under Pixabay.

So, we continue…

Our "snowbird" neighbors have finally just returned from Florida. After months of their worrying about the hazard of air travel, they're here–after betting their lives on the blind hope that the risks of getting here might be less than staying on any longer in that State.

From another recent flight out of Florida, three passengers who tested positive for Covid-19, when arriving locally, set off alarms for tracing, testing and, where needed, treatment of anyone associated with the flight.

Alarming increases in notified new cases of Covid-19 are occurring daily in two-thirds of U.S. states, including Florida. Patients, healthcare workers, and a host of "front-line" people providing services to the community face the prospect of no let up, and likely worse to come.

When life, liberty, happiness, and peace of mind are breached all at once, the simple question is: "Which leaders are doing what to protect the people?"

Especially in these times, it's a question of what elected representatives are doing for "we," rather than her or him. It's a question not of what she or he is saying, but what she or he does.

Clearing up who are the "we" people and who are the "me" people helps a lot. Not that we didn't notice this in people at times. But taking a closer look is like putting on 3D-glasses in a movie!

Then we readily see, in sharp relief, the politician who, convicted of felonies, gets elected anyway–clearly, he and his supporters never heard from my Irish grandfather, who'd quip that there are no degrees of honesty!

Or the political operative who seems to think it's still ok to manipulate voting, or the garbage collector who leaves your garbage bin full on your front driveway because he couldn't work his truck's lift mechanism properly, or the neighbor's air conditioning contractor who puts his advertising sign on our front lawn instead of the neighbor's, so his company name gets a better view from the street (clearly, I need to get out more...)

Could continue endlessly of course on who thinks of "we" or "me"– say, "road rage" individuals, the open-carry and AR-15 crowds, etc. Anyway, for the big and small, the "we" or "me" filter sure clarifies.

Then, since at least 1998, there's the political party that has gathered research data from electrodes on voters, in focus groups that they euphemistically call "dial sessions." They look for bio-reactions to political comments, to determine the "right words" to use uniformly in talking points across the party. What bucket of deceptive self-interest do you put that in?

But wait, what about #MeToo? Easy... this is a collective "we," who seek redress from the hormone driven "Me" crowd. Or Black Lives

Matter or similar movements? Again, when these are a collective "we," who seek remedy from the driven "Me" crowd, you can feel good with it.

How clarifying our language is. What visiting Martian would believe a couple of pronouns could clarify so much—just by looking afresh through the filter of "we" or "me"?

That's the only choice really in any election. Who cares to do for we the people?

July 12, 2020

To Speak Out!

The Platypus sings of the antediluvian days
Kangaroo frontis by Unknown artist from *Dot and the Kangaroo,* 1899.
This image is in the Public Domain {{PD-US-expired}}
https://commons.wikimedia.org/wiki/Dot_and_the_Kangaroo#
/media/File:Kangaroo_frontis.jpg

True leaders advance the common good, using "...truthful, lawful, and just speech"–as recommended for more than 2,400 years.

My new book, *Australians Speak Out: Persuasive Language Styles,* assesses persuasive language styles in the speeches and writing of leaders in one modern nation, who got it right. These leaders had to speak directly, laconically at times, and use plain talk to hold the attention of audiences. The book is packed with examples of **how extraordinary speakers and writers use ordinary words to make representative democracy thrive**–with creative uses of metaphor, humor, polemic, *anaphora,* and political jargon—all with rhetorical flair. It describes the persuasive language of some notable Australians, from the 1890s to the 21st century. Detailed are ways that word choice, sentence shape, and passage development enable successful arguments for change.

Living in the United States through the absurdity of the initial handling of Covid and a remarkable election, I kept some perspective by exploring a rich heritage of extraordinary Australians who advocate social and political change—completing the book while intense fights for democracy continue throughout the world.

Speaking Up

In Australia, where the anti-hero is revered, leaders have to speak up and speak out in individual ways. When the Olympics were held here, on the night before the race, the blue line marking the marathon course was erased from one section of the course—the next morning to be found repainted running up to one pub door and out from another.

It's the same nation where, amid the Covid pandemic early in 2020, photos spontaneously appeared on the Internet of suburban dwellers dressed in startling costumes as superheroes, zombies, grotesques, princesses, etc., just to roll out their wheelie garbage bins to the front of their homes for collection. Australians deal with the absurd with a developed sense of humor and a sense of independence.

At a time when truthful, lawful, and just speech is needed more than ever, the book takes a fresh look at how prime ministers, other community leaders, and advocates of change attract attention and move people to action.

Australians Speak Out reveals the persuasive language of notable Australians whose advocacy helped to
  * Federate the colonies of Britain in the South Pacific as one nation
  * Make Australian women among the first to be able to vote, in 1902
  * Appeal to the people of the United States for wartime support
  * Establish rights for First Nations
  * Challenge sexism

* Reform laws to respect human rights
* Control guns
* Deal with the Covid pandemic

and advance many other causes by appealing to our reason and emotions. For ready access, a selection of notable speeches and writing is included.

Direct Appeals

Looking closely at the language of more than 20 notable Australians, who helped to transform the colonies of Britain into a multicultural nation on the world stage, brought surprises along with expected familiarity. Familiar now to relatively few is the plea during World War II to strengthen the partnership of the United States and Australia to defeat foreign aggression in the Pacific—from prime minister John Curtin, speaking via radio directly to the people of the United States.

Perhaps more readily recalled are prime ministers Sir Robert Menzies and Gough Whitlam, who respectively committed and removed Australian troops in support of the United States in Vietnam. Or Germaine Greer provocatively addressing women's rights at the National Press Club in Washington DC in 1971—while promoting publication of *The Female Eunuch*, with the persuasive language that she used in her book reviewed here.

Advocacy for Action

Surprising to some might be the powerful language of Louisa Lawson's social activism, which spearheaded women's right to vote on the same terms as men in 1902; and yet peoples in the First Nations were unable to vote until 1962.

The disturbing treatment of First Nations was finally officially acknowledged during the term of the reform prime minister Gough Whitlam, elected in 1972, and in the landmark speeches of prime ministers Paul Keating (1992) and Kevin Rudd (2008). Yet, still unaddressed were key rights for First Nations strongly advocated from the late 20th century, by activists like Oodgeroo Noonuccal [Kath Walker] and Kevin Gilbert, whose speeches are reviewed in the book.

Also assessed are the remarkable speeches and writing of the former Justice of the High Court, Michael Kirby, who recalls the inspiration that Eleanor Roosevelt brought to schoolchildren through her visit to Sydney in 1944—and to his own life-long commitment of reforming laws to respect human rights. And, how The Right Honourable Lord Mayor of Brisbane, Sallyanne Atkinson, invited British royalty who were present to join Brisbane residents in "our party," to celebrate the City's coming of age at the opening of World Expo '88.

From more recent times, there are powerful, and perhaps surprising speeches. These include prime minister John Howard's address to transform gun ownership nationally, little more than a month after the Port Arthur massacre in 1996, and prime minister Julia Gillard's address to parliament in 2012 in her powerful objection to sexism, which resonated around the world—to prime minister Morrison's brief but reassuring plan to deal with the Covid pandemic.

For anyone interested in a close look at words that appeal to audiences—words that are authentic and move hearts and minds!

April 7, 2022

.0001%

The Bookworm
by Carl Spritzweg (1808-1885), Museum Georg Schäfer.
This image is in the Public Domain {{PD-US-expired}}
https://en.wikipedia.org/wiki/File:Carl_Spitzweg_021.jpg

Policy wonks long believed healthcare delivery to be governed by considerations of Access, Quality, and Cost—and, that it was possible to address any two, but not all three satisfactorily. Policy prophecy can be self-fulfilling, or worse, as we now know from endless hours dealing with health insurance companies, pharmacies, and the others fiddling in this space.

Hype among policy determiners often has self-fulfilling effects. In the mass media, for example, the preoccupation with ratings and advertising sales has predetermined the constraints within which the most creative editors, journalists, and others are bound to work. Progressively, added to the mix are the effects of new tech.

The editor-in-chief of the newspapers in my hometown, Harry Gordon, contrasted how print and broadcast news media might report on Moses receiving the Ten Commandments. Gordon wrote the newspaper version of this story as "Moses came down from the mountain today with Ten Commandments. These are… [with the ten guides-to-life described]." He projected that the broadcast news would be "Moses has delivered Ten Commandments, two of which are…"

How social media might relate this news is anyone's guess. But more interesting is the hype that tech fashion has self-perpetuated, as well as its long-term effects.

Over a decade ago, the CEO of an early online search firm shared his surprise with me that his teenage daughter showed no interest in participating in that rite-of-passage of earlier generations, of proving skills enough to obtain a driver's license. Her answer, living in central city, was to text a friend, if she wanted a ride to go somewhere; and not long afterwards, Uber was born!

Now, it's reported that, in a nation whose people seem otherwise sensible, the National Library of New Zealand is set to "de-accession" over 600,000 "Overseas" Books collections, including Shakespeare, Cervantes [that should stop future tilting at the windmills of wonks!], all the classics, and much more. Oh, and just about any other non-New Zealand literature you might (or might not) be encyclopedic enough to remember. Some policy wonking, eh?! Even the shortlist for the chop, identified in a *World of the Written Word* blog post on July 9, is remarkable.

Interestingly, the "Internet Library" chosen as New Zealand's substitute knowledge repository, unlike a physical library, appears not to compensate authors still in copyright, or their publishers' production efforts—no mention of either buying or re-buying books, as other libraries do, much less per page lending and payment systems so common elsewhere. Naturally, publishers and at least one author association are mounting legal challenges to the presumptions underlying the approach, with proceedings still winding through the courts.

Also not considered important apparently are the realities of digital storage decay, or who will really take care of the periodic re-"saving" that will be needed for such mountains of information in yet-to-be developed new digital formats. No indication that the so-called Internet pirates discussed in a more recent blog post, who are to be the substitute caretakers of this knowledge resource of New Zealand, have any concern about this. Nor any mention of other consequent losses from them or the library policy wonks, who seem fine about glossing over losses to the nation in deciding on their approach.

Such wonks will likely remain enamored with the idyllic fantasy portrayed by sci-fi movie actors, who talk to computers to retrieve any information that the movie script, written by someone else, has told them how to request.

At the risk of sounding even more like a dinosaur, the other, even-bigger effect that pops up regularly in the news is the ambiguous security of our "wired and wireless" controlled infrastructure for power, transport, health systems, media, etc., national and personal, which we are all governed by. Amid seemingly uncontrolled forces, there are some things we can do.

A key "to do" was crystallized in the years I worked alongside two very talented undergraduate computing students, to deliver computer-coding competitions, we called "hackathons." Within this tech-set, social media was gospel for every purpose, except to get geeks to enroll in the (free) computer-coding competition.

Which is where the title of today's blog post comes from. ".0001%" was roughly the percentage return, calculated over the years, of the actual enrollment in our "hackathons" that resulted from social media, in a highly tech community—in other words, insignificant in this group. Of course, with different resources to drive social media, including automated systems and expensive demographic data, and/or with very much larger population groups, and/or with physiological pre-testing of messages, and/or, etc., etc., others do better.

Just have a look at the election exploitations via social media in the United States and other countries, where the first or strongest in a territory/nation with relatively developed resources has done well–especially where the opponent gears up little or not at all with social media, in offense or defense. But the distance between results and hype in our modestly resourced "hackathon" marketing efforts always stunned us.

As you might have guessed, what worked to engage participants in our "hackathon" competition, and in all the other big computer-coding events we surveyed in Michigan, Boston, and elsewhere, was word-of-mouth/person-to-person. As my tech-student colleagues found, what worked was standing, day-after-day, in the university quad and food court, handing out flyers–inviting personally–and, yes, email still lives... with personalized email follow-up.

This also applies to dismantling propaganda, by restoring dialog. Or, nurturing critical thinking (Socratic dialog doesn't seem to fly too well on social media). Or inviting others to join a cause. Zoom calls in these times are helpful.

It will be best for us all the soonest and more completely that the United States, or for that matter any nation or community, finds person-to-person ways to further enliven the community interactions that shape democratic strength.

[FOOTNOTE UPDATE--At the end of November 2021, a reprieve for an unspecified time from the proposed action of the National Library of NZ was announced–possibly due to the legal uncertainties mentioned above, along with potential embroilment in the likely long-winded and expensive legal proceedings mounted by publishers and author organizations against the so-called "Internet Library" in the United States.]

July 20, 2021

Democracy

To Strengthen Democracy

Narcissus
By Caravaggio (1571-1610). This image is in the Public Domain {{PD-US-expired}}
https://commons.wikimedia.org/wiki/File:Narcissus-Caravaggio_(1594-96).jpg

If imitation is the sincerest form of flattery, how hugely ironic it is that phony populists swim in a sea of self-adulation, obsessively interested only in themselves; narcissistic in their ignorance that George Orwell long ago illustrated how to tear down trash-talk to restore truth, and Jacques Ellul alerted us to both the dangers and limits of propaganda.

Like many of us today, Orwell and Ellul had their fill of wannabe leaders wanting to snatch up control of governments and freedoms. And we hardly need reminding of the horrors that the phony leaders caused then.

During the upsurge in phony populism more recently, it's been healthy and helpful to use the mute button on nonsense claims, or switch TV channels, or turn off the tech, or question presumptions in the too-often-repeated outrages.

It's understandable to wonder where the mute button is to counter propaganda more widely. We dampen nonsense on television this way, why not other trash-talk? And why do mainstream and social media so like to magnify manufactured outrage?

When a fringe-mob violently tried to overthrow democratic government in the United States almost seven months ago, many of us were more than tired of the phony tirades and trash-talk. By then, manufactured outrages often dominated public communications.

Orwell and Ellul had warned about the use of media to engulf us in a swell of swill. Ellul noted that propagandists win by denying freedom of thought. And, with fashion, rumors, and propagators of weird social beliefs aided and abetted by some unprofessional news-folks and social media, of course we'll always be targets of propagandists.

To help swim the sea of propaganda, with its hidden currents and rips, and to encourage the critical thinking needed to do so, Jacques Ellul outlined what enables propaganda. He provided relatively few specifics on what we each might do to counter propaganda, as Randal Marlin pointed out in a recent blog post (Marlin, 2021). Ellul sought to stimulate, not dictate our thinking. His thoroughly exploring principles and practices remains useful though, to help swim across the tidal rips of propaganda to reach a better destination.

One of Orwell's contributions was to help us scrutinize language, to look for the tells that identify the self-interested wannabe controllers of thinking. He also explained how to deal with their language, which was especially well-outlined in his famous essay, "Politics and the English Language"–first published in 1946, and still well worth the (re-)read.

As daily life gets engulfed in the swill on digital devices and other products of the technological age that we welcome into our lives, it becomes increasingly important to enlarge commitments to critical thinking. Educators have a role here, but the declines in teaching logic and the already crowded educational curricula mean that logic and other life skills like civility, or information literacy, or financial management, or the law will be formal educational experiences beyond the reach of many.

So, it is up to each of us to build defenses and offensives to dismantle propaganda. Check out other postings on this blog for some "to do's" to counter propaganda, and/or look into Randal Marlin's excellent *Propaganda and the Ethics of Persuasion*.

Plenty to be concerned about, with the continuously rising impact of technology on what we see, hear, and do, as well as the ongoing efforts of wannabe leaders pretending to be democratic, who aim to control people directly, or through legislative sleights of hand.

July 30, 2021

Speaking Out

Dr. Martin Luther King Jr. giving his "I Have a Dream" speech at the Lincoln Memorial during the March on Washington, D.C., on August 28, 1963

by Rowland Scherman (1937-) National Archive.
This image is in the Public Domain {{PD-USGov-USIA}}
https://commons.wikimedia.org/wiki/File:Martin_Luther_King_-_March_on_Washington.jpg

"I have a dream that my four little children will one day live in a nation where they will not be judged by the color of their skin but by the content of their character."

Democracy has a long association with communication. In Montesquieu's view, the durability of free government depends on a nation's capacity for self-correction.

Citizens judge political events from the reports of electronic media, newspapers, or politicians themselves. We have few guidelines for assessing the value of such reports.

Educational curricula need much revision to ensure effective teaching of civics.

Concurrently, it is important to develop in individuals some key virtues of Western civilization, such as **justice, temperance, courage,** and **wisdom.** The teaching of writing and public talk must develop the responsible principles learned from a rich legacy of thoughtful speakers and commentators.

As from the earliest times, improved understanding of **what makes public talk effective** will empower future *rhetors* to speak out, as the best assurance that democracy will thrive.

Conscious of the resonant comment from George Orwell that "political language is designed to make lies sound truthful and murder respectable," **a public who listens and speaks out is the root of democracy.**

June 3, 2020

Civil Civics

Old Glory
by US Air Force. This image is in the Public Domain {{PD-USGov-Military}}
https://commons.wikimedia.org/wiki/File:Old_Glory_(15102558108).jpg

Just when the need is great, this month more than 300 educators from across the United States delivered a report and roadmap targeted to enhance *Educating for American Democracy*, for K-12 education in history and civics.

This remarkable effort, involving wide-ranging consultations for over a year, resulted from the support of the National Endowment for the Humanities and the US Department of Education to address the serious need in this country for better understandings of civics. This is an ambitious roadmap, providing national guidelines that invite responses for state, local, tribal, county, and district-level solutions to how the roadmap gets implemented.

A key educational goal is to enable future generations to be effective citizens and decision-makers, by seeing their part in shaping the future.

During a national forum to launch the roadmap, Harvard Professor Jane Kamensky spoke to the purpose of equipping students "to ask hard questions, and learn to answer them effectively from evidence, and by deliberating about that evidence even with people who disagree with you, maybe especially with people who disagree with you."

The roadmap outlines a carefully considered approach to improve understandings and involvement in civic decision-making. It incorporates historical content and the stories of the nation's institutions and democratic concepts, as well as considering "people with contemporary debates and possibilities."

This effort to strengthen the foundation in the United States for citizen participation in civic decision-making will be ongoing. It provides a welcome step to address the well-documented need to improve history and civics education, to help sustain democracy.

Note

_____ (2021), *Educating for American Democracy Project*, https://www.educatingforamericandemocracy.org

March 22, 2021

Remembrance

World War I veteran Joseph Ambrose, 86,
at Vietnam Veterans Memorial in 1982
by Mickey Sanborn, Department of Defense, National Archives.
This image is in the Public Domain {{PD-USGov-Military}}
https://commons.wikimedia.org/wiki/File:World_War_I_veteran_Joseph_Ambrose,_86,_at_the_dedic
ation_day_parade_for_the_Vietnam_Veterans_Memorial_in_1982.jpg

United through invisible links stronger than titanium are people who live in genuine democracies worldwide. Regardless of local or national differences, consistently valued is the appreciation of freedom.

At certain times of the year, at home, school, or workplace, we pay tribute to all who have saved so many countries from tyranny. We pause in memory of the veterans who served, so that we live free; and we experience again the truth that sanity may rule, when tyrants don't.

This year at 11 am, on the eleventh day of the eleventh month, the "complete suspension of all our normal activities" to observe two-minutes of silence felt especially significant, with remembrance genuinely reaffirmed at the national level.

Likewise, much appreciated from across the miles was a friend's email with spectacular photos attached of poppies projected onto the shell-like sails of the Sydney Opera House.

The email referred also to what *Country Life* in the UK has described as "a mammoth new work recounting the First World War, week by week... a rich tapestry of courage, camaraderie and love." The four-volume publication titled *As We Were*, at over 2,200 pages by David Hargreaves and Margaret-Louise O'Keeffe, reminds of the pain, dignity, and contradictions of a war that was touted to end all wars. This work is well reviewed by David Crane in *The Spectator* on 27 February 2021.

The huge loss and efforts in 20th century wars especially, along with the losses and sacrifices of veterans in too many wars since, link us in a legacy of commitment to sustain freedoms of thought, speech, and association—within democracies. **Lest we forget.**

November 15, 2021

Speak Read Write Vote

Roots of Democracy
First four American stamps, the 1977 Americana Series
by United States Postal Service. This image is in the Public Domain {{PD-USGov}}
https://commons.wikimedia.org/wiki/File:Americanaseries.jpg

"Safety from external danger is the most powerful director of national conduct. Even the ardent love of liberty will, after a time, give way to its dictates."
–Alexander Hamilton, *The Federalist* No. 8, 20 November 1787

Regardless of such wisdom, it was for much too long that otherwise sensible people slept through Churchill's alerts to the danger of tyrants, less than a century ago. Who will neuter the propaganda weapon of today's wannabe-tyrants, foreign or domestic?

If the legal profession's clichéd explanation that shouting "Fire" in a crowded movie theater is not acceptable, how is it that propaganda threatening democracy is? Is this propaganda rightly protected speech?

At the very least, we need progress to prosecute propagandists driving "schemes and artifices" for mail or wire fraud, or perjury, or defamation, or any other actionable threat I'm not thinking of. When gaming the rule of law is the rule of play, will rational problem-solvers-at-law ever advance actions at a speed to meet the need?

With bizarre mirages of propagandists filling the airwaves, some more bright lights are needed in the media to counter what's wildly opposite to reality. The mirages of crazies are certainly not diverted by media amplifications of them.

Perhaps one day, we'll again encounter worthwhile puzzles, instead of addressing how so many people can believe the unbelievable. And maybe it's time to stop looking at hucksters as if they operate by the norms of normal people. To defeat a twisted mind, we don't need to be twisted, but we'd better be able to project the next move—and get ahead of it.

Some individuals spend a lifetime's energy on coming up with distorted talk to smooth over distorted actions. Savvy people get this and have a nose to detect the grifter and pretender. Even household pets might be inspiration here—they've retained senses to detect looming danger.

How much longer are we all to stand for glacial movements toward potential accountability? Sustaining democracy requires the wide-awake actions of "we the people."

August 31, 2022

Now Is the Time

Spoof of the Statue of Liberty
by LeoFed. This image is in the Public Domain.
https://commons.wikimedia.org/wiki/File:Vader-statue-of-liberty.jpg

With the many anti-democracy propagandists still generally not held accountable, it seems one of the extra steps now needed to be able to vote in the United States is to check again that you are enrolled—well before turning up at the polling booth or mailing in your vote.

Best check now whether you're still enrolled. If not, you're not alone.

As the autocrats propagandize, "a lot of people are saying" that they are finding themselves unenrolled, or with changed party affiliation, or other new inaccuracies. One clue to this might be receiving mail from your local elections board at your address, directed to the "current resident."

Thanks to the continued adoption of the playbook of autocrats, it looks like "Darth Vader's" servants might be continuing to amp up the direct interference in the electoral process that's become a regular challenge elsewhere, especially for some European democracies.

For good reason, for example, the Netherlands has advanced most elections since November 2006 to be by paper ballot.

Now there's a blasphemy the technology evangelists here aren't likely to adopt.

September 16, 2022

Truth, Law, and Justice

Beyond Heavens

Orion Belt
by Davide De Martin, Digitized Sky Survey, ESA/ESO/NASA FITS Liberator.
This image is in the Public Domain {{PD-USGov-NASA}}
https://commons.wikimedia.org/wiki/File:Orion_Belt.jpg

Growing up with astronomy as an interest was some preparation for dealing with current fantasies in public communications. Although astronomers see very little of the oblivion they relentlessly probe, they often develop remarkable theories to understand the unexplained and what might feel unexplainable.

Gazing into the heavens is serious business though. These generally trusted scientists don't confuse theory and myth. For example, shining brightly in the night sky is the welcome constancy of the planet Venus. Named for the goddess of love, a tangible value of Venus is to help navigators by pointing to the constellation Orion, the hunter.

Orion, as we know, is also something of a bright light in mythology, who has attracted varying interpretations. He had an encounter with Artemis, during his quest for one of the seven nymphs sent by Zeus to guard her. Since Artemis is the Greek equivalent of the Romans' Diana, and both were goddesses of the hunt, it's your choice on who to follow.

This was fascinating to the Ancients and also got the interest of some astronomers with dual devotion to mythology and science. The ancient Greeks and Romans believed the gods played with we mere mortals. In subsequent centuries, apart from the withering vine of astrology and the never-say-die occultists, mostly astronomers and other mere mortals have agreed that the gods and their colluder representations in the sky above us are illusions.

Astronomers see that the forces and matter of the real universe are massive, observable, magnificent, and often beyond our grasp. At first glance, the scale might feel similar when viewing the fantasies of stoked fears, greed, and even apathy that perpetuate populist politics. The myths are large, the outrage of conspiracy theories is galactic in size, as well as both colorful and gaseous in composition. Just looking at and recording their aberration sure doesn't help.

At human scale, comedy can be a usefully quick comeback. More enduring is to build systematic education in both values and analytic ability. Regardless of whether or not what our leaders say is truthful, lawful, and just, "voters are increasingly drawn to leaders who can make difficult, complex problems easier to understand with intuitive, confident answers." This is according to a 2019 worldwide study of long-term trends in politics and culture, cited in *Proceedings National Academy of Sciences* (Vol. 116, No. 9, pp. 3476-81) edited by Stephen Pinker. This study further notes that a decline in analytical communication style began around 1980.

Do I need to mention again that this was noted to be a worldwide trend (at least, in English-speaking nations)? So, the time for action is yesterday.

Of course, if the world wants to keep waiting out the passing of the equivalent of the Horsemen of the Apocalypse, that's an option, just not a good one in these precipitous times.

November 29, 2020

Trouble with Theory

Supreme Court, Washington DC
By David Dugan. This image is licensed under CCA-SA-3.0 Unported.
https://commons.wikimedia.org/wiki/File:15-23-0154,_Supreme_Court_-_panoramio.jpg

At the outset, just for the record, I'm committed to theory and putting theory to work. Yet, whether "relentless public scrutiny" is just a fallacy of political theorists is about to be clarified in the United States.

We're soon to see what happens to democracy too. Coming days, weeks and maybe years will produce an uncountable number of words about this. Whatever happens, divergent ideas of popular democracy, liberal democracy, and representative democracy will likely get thrown around with abandon.

Although what we mean by democracy is a legitimate concern, perhaps the more immediate question should be who will do something useful about two especially serious failures of theory?

Firstly, what will you do to push back on the too-frequent failure of the so-called "guardrails" of public accountability?

Perhaps someone can tell me where the prosecution of public corruption in the United States is timely, or has worked effectively? Most often this appears no longer expected in this oh-so-sensitive-to-popular-sentiment political climate.

Are voters supposed to believe that the multiple statute books federally, for example, really lack "teeth" or require such difficult proof that prosecution really is worthless?

Proof of value should be performance in use, not leaving needed laws sitting in the statute books. Goodness knows there's been plenty of malfeasance and corruption to warrant prosecutions in recent times.

Political theorists continue to write about their interviews with leading political and government pragmatists. Then, they republish as largely unqualified "wisdom" what they're told about artifacts called "guardrails," which appear to be so valued that they can't be tainted by use.

Meantime, the numbers of whistleblowers and others leaving public service with careers and personal safety in tatters for speaking out just continue to soar.

If a law is not useful enough to be used, the time on theorizing could be better spent dreaming up some provisions that even flawed public figures would have to use—or else, spend some time dreaming up how such failing "representatives" of the public might be removed quickly but fairly by the population if they don't. Apparently, that's a problem worthy of a legal-political science equivalent of Einstein.

Secondly, what will you do to find and urge the elected politicians who do care to do something better, to help

1. Educate everyone about detecting and calling out propaganda.

2. Codify remedies to the multiple deficiencies of norms and regulations to protect the rule of law.

3. Educate everyone about putting civics to use?

I'm sure you could add much to this list, as I could, but these are gargantuan enough for a start.

Here we all are now, stuck in the effects of blatant failures in accountability, and "we, the people" remain caught in the consequences of bad actors.

While such matters are still richly fermenting, before much further deluge of theoretical posturing, it's time to demand action.

December 2, 2020

Accountability

The Constitution of the United States of America
by Bluszczokrzew, Constitution_Pg104_AC.jpg: Constitution Convention (retouched).
This image is in the Public Domain {{PD-USGov}}
https://commons.wikimedia.org/wiki/File:Constitution_We_the_People.jpg

"The most important thing to hear in communication is what isn't said." –Peter Drucker

Some time ago, with the aim of getting attention in a lunchtime talk to a group of public relations folks, I began by sharing a comment of one of their clients when he learned of my scheduled talk. "P.R." he'd said, "is hokum and deception. It's the preserve of charlatans and magicians!!"

After I delivered this "gem" to the PR practitioners, amid the unexpected cheers and applause that they responded with, I quickly modified how to talk with them about communication.

We are in an era when "P.R." doesn't represent Public Responsibility, if it ever did.

Among the serious challenges facing citizens in representative democracies are the **24/7 news cycle** and **huge paid propaganda.** For even the most responsible elected representatives, "PR" (the public relations version) is a greater magnet than ever before–especially at election time. On the television talk shows, we occasionally see this in an overly appreciative glance (and sometimes over-effusive thanks) given by an elected representative to a television host.

The PR of Congressional Hearings and investigations and follow-up interviews do get tiresome when there's no result. All that endless handwringing, the "dodges" and refinements might provide media moments for some elected representatives. Too often, these confuse the essential matter, namely securing remedy of a crooked action.

Electors should expect accountability for corruption and malfeasance—including punishment, intervention, and removal where appropriate. Now, not later.

It's time to recognize that sticking solely with the strategies of trading words and pursuing legal messes does not serve representative democracy. It's important to recognize that fighting bad actors on these terms, where they're smart, will rarely work. It's time to <u>turn off funds and resources</u> to bad actors—not just talk about it on TV.

What democracy needs more than ever is not PR talk, but genuine callings to account. The Westminster system long ago formalized the role of the Opposition. Each government minister (cabinet member) has a well-briefed competent counterpart as a "Shadow" cabinet member in the opposition party. The role includes keeping the cabinet member as honest as possible on specifics (as well as being up-to-speed when the government changes). Doesn't always work as desired, but it helps.

In the "Washington system," it looks like the checks and balances that were designed thoughtfully by the Founders for different times only work (like most rules and norms) in some circumstances… unsurprisingly, when they're encompassing enough for effective people to make use of them.

Today, it's plain to a near-sighted bandicoot, that we're not in such a circumstance. Substantial changes to laws and norms are needed, along with action from elected representatives and anyone else positioned to take action, instead of waiting for the mythical someone else to step forward.

In the meantime, with so much awry, as the ever-continuing revelations and memes show, the challenge is what to do and when.

Anytime confusion rules, it's best to go back to basic principles. A basic principle of democracy is "A public who listen and speak out." When you're fed up with the level of preoccupation with PR, here are some thoughts to help set your action plan, to let it be known that there is a public who cares:

1. Do get personal (nicely) with your elected representatives - NOW is the time; none better than during election campaigns. Send a letter and make a phone call (not an email or tweet!) to question what she or he is doing about what you care about. In the lead up to an election, once a week on different issues might keep attention, if you're comfortable with this (she or he does work for you). Ask for a specific answer each time!

2. If you're a joiner, join an action group that puts pressure and expects results from elected representatives. United States citizens are still in the top levels of volunteer participation (however you measure it). The 2018 Volunteering in America report found that 77.34 million adults (30.3 percent) volunteered through an organization that year.

3. Make the effort to become familiar with and use Freedom of Information (FOI) legislation to learn what government is really doing on the matters you care about.

Here's a quick list of some countries with FOI legislation and when it was enacted:

United States, France, Denmark, Finland, Sweden, Netherlands (all by 1967)
Australia, New Zealand (in 1982)
Canada (in 1983)
United Kingdom (2000 to 2001)
Scotland (2005)

Elected representatives might eventually recognize that "the people" know more and expect better. Perhaps the norm of public handwringing will **shift to getting results.**

July 1, 2020

Letters of Law

Humpty Dumpty
by Christopher Wood, Hunter Valley Gardens, 29 December 2009.
This image is licensed under CCA-SA 3.0 Unported.
https://commons.wikimedia.org/wiki/File:08._Humpty_Dumpty_-_panoramio.jpg

A foundation for a fair application of the law requires the interpretation of law and facts. How judges and juries interpret words, in statutes, or case reports, or the description of facts, is central to the effective operation of the legal system.

Recent articles which I'm grateful a friend pointed out, in *Science* and in the Harvard and Yale law journals, look at the varying ways that judges, juries, the legal profession, and everyday people interpret the meaning of words. It's perhaps no surprise that unlike Humpty Dumpty in *Alice in Wonderland*, for whom a word meant whatever he chose for it, the law seeks more consistency.

What should rock the legal profession and concern everyone is how much juries can differ from judges about the meaning of words. It might be no surprise that how judges and juries interpret words can differ greatly. Within a case, or between successive cases, the character of language permits varying interpretations of meaning.

This is so, even with the efforts to apply the law's special rules that seek clarity and consistency, including various uses of "canons of interpretation, relevant context, or the text's purpose." In one of the articles, Kevin Tobia from Georgetown Law noted that Justice Frankfurter had remarked "Anything that is written may present a problem of meaning... The problem derives from the very nature of words." People in general, as well as students of language, intuitively understand this.

And so do others in the legal profession, which doubtless helps to add fuel to ongoing debates about originalism or other legal niceties of interpretation. Just two of the more interesting implications stimulated beyond these articles include firstly, how juries interpret *deceit* and secondly, the challenge to prove *intent*.

On the first for example, as I understand it, when deceit enables an agreement that, arguably, does not go to the heart of the contract (as well as in some other circumstances), juries that apply "commonsense consent" (rather than some legal norms), tend to side with the perpetrator rather than the victim. Roseanna Sommers, from University of Michigan Law, explains the concepts, some psychological experiments that seek to explain such interpretations, and what this means for the law itself.

More broadly, the layperson's tolerance for deceit might also at least partly explain why voters will (re-)elect politicians charged with or convicted of criminal offenses. While such understanding is good to have, it's not any less disturbing, especially in the current context in the United States.

On the second challenge, as difficult as the tangled interpretations of consent continue to be, it could be helpful if the authors of these articles in the future paid more attention to *intent*. In particular, it would be very helpful to look at how the law's normative definitions for proof of intent cause trouble–especially in criminal law.

It's possible that any "commonsense blindness" to deceit might also contribute to the difficulties of proving intent in court. And, likely such "commonsense" fuels the more general tolerance of the fraudulent behavior of some public figures, for example, who are perpetually engaged in attempted corruption of the electoral system and justice through frivolous litigation. Likewise, the difficulty of proving intent probably contributes to the failure to prosecute the bad actions of public figures, which further debilitates representative democracy.

Let's remember that juries supposedly consist of everyday persons drawn from the community, on the democratic principle that any person's case should be judged by one's peers—as a holdover and ongoing symbolic and substantive statement of true populism over the monarchy or other autocratic rule.

Valuable as these articles are to anyone with an inclination toward the brain-bending needed for legal semantics, their largest consequences will probably emerge through teasing out further commonsense meanings in the interconnection of legal interpretation with people's lives.

The importance of the work of these scholars cannot be overstated. And the concluding remarks of Sommers's longer 2020 article, located at pp. 2306-7, are especially interesting perspective. Each author inherently puts in question some basic assumptions about the realities of how the law operates to benefit civil society.

Notes

Roseanna Sommers (2021), "Experimental Jurisprudence: Psychologists Probe Lay Understandings of Legal Constructs," *Science,* Vol 373:6553, 23 July, pp. 394-5

Roseanna Sommers (2020), "Commonsense Consent," *Yale Law Journal,* Vol 129:8, pp. 2232-307

Kevin P. Tobia (2020), "Testing Ordinary Meaning," *Harvard Law Review,* Vol 134:726, pp. 727-806

August 19, 2021

Media

Fall in the Suburbs

Cinnamon Bear Cub Tackles Garbage
by Gillfoto is licensed under CCA-SA 4.0 International.
https://commons.wikimedia.org/wiki/File:Cinnamon_Bear_Cub_Garbage_22.jpg

At this time each year with foliage fallen, in the early morning half-light, animated shadows take the shape of deer hearing a noise inaudible to others, and, looking up from grazing on their favorite garden beds, turn tail to scatter, clattering across the bitumen of neighborhood roads. In this season, human suburbanites bring out a bevy of birdfeeders, multiplying the offerings of seed and suet to help the birds, and the inevitable squirrels and chipmunks, through the winter.

On sunny days, a shadow sensed overhead causes birds and the smaller creatures to freeze like stalagmites, alert to a predator hawk's survey before its dive-through swoop. At times, a bear, or bobcat, or quick red fox will be glimpsed crossing the fallen leaves, attending to pre-winter foraging. Hunkering down and preparing for what's to come are instincts strongly sustained by suburbanized animals—and this is also somewhat true of their human neighbors.

A not-so-mythical Neighbor Jones attends to outdoor chores to prepare home for winter. Apparently a keen role model, Jones keeps right up to date with the latest garden tools, gutter guards, and any advertised gizmo needed for such responsibility. A dimming memory of Aesop's fables, or James Thurber's stories, fables, and cartoons, or quips of Ogden Nash might keep some suburbanites' feet on the ground, but Jones captures currency with TV and social media clicks and swipes.

This very modern commander of what is popular frequently forages the advertised specials, to keep ahead of the outdated. With dopamine that advertisements and media have stimulated in the brain for more seasons than remembered, Jones is ritually separated from conscious thought. Gilbert and Sullivan's very model modern-major-general would rank lowly in an award for mindlessness compared with this embodiment of the media's key goal, which is to have more people diligently spending more time on the media.

So runs the theme of an intriguing book, *Veils of Distortion: How the News Media Warp Our Minds*, recently launched by a practicing journalist, John Zada. This is not a new suggestion. Vance Packard was a canary in the coal mine, so to speak, pointing to practices in subliminal advertising in *The Hidden Persuaders* in the 1950s. In the next decade, Jacques Ellul alerted to the power of social propaganda, which predisposes us to respond to the most unremarkable drivel. And many more since.

What's refreshing within Zada's insights, beyond his being employed in the news media and daring to critique the news media, are observations on how it is that what gets treated as news are aberrations from real life for most people—and, how this news sets an increased appetite for reports of the bizarre, the dangerous, and the outlier, which ever since people existed, we are keen to know about. Zada describes a variety of added touches that degrade the news as "info-tainment."

He suggests that this "news" crowds out reality. The news media just keep on obsessively covering mainly outlier incidents to infer a besieged, beleaguered world, contrary to what most people might ever experience. And, for all this churning invention of an apocalyptic fantasy, news media outlets in fierce competition with each other are competing for an ever-diminishing pool of followers, as droves of potential readers and viewers choose to spend time elsewhere—little wonder!

Yet, without the persistently professional investigations of journalists, much malfeasance of elected officials would never be known. And, journalists deploy information gathering and writing abilities within standards of the profession, media management, audience interests, and other constraints that would paralyze many people. Their continuous discovering and shaping for us items truly fit to print or to broadcast is an ever changing landscape, ever demanding on talent, patience, persistence, politeness, and a host of other positive human qualities.

Zada seeks to avoid taking cheap shots at his colleagues though. He defines types of "fake news" precisely to include disinformation. And he alerts to the supercharged impact by which the news media are servants of conspirators and other disinformation merchants, by obligingly amplifying their existence, activities, and messages. Such "reporters," hyped by dopamine of their own making, highlight extreme details of disinformation merchants to ensure a "news piece" gets passed through the news organization's internal gatekeepers for publication or broadcast.

Zada points out that Aric Toler has noted news media magnify the reach of disinformation "way beyond anything Moscow could achieve by itself." Likewise, touched on is how news media ever so regularly cover grifter and charlatan politicians, massively expanding the reach of their propaganda. He points to the role of PR as propaganda and many other aspects of "churnalism" in the "news factory."

While this book mainly probes a great many examples of the distortions to offer diagnosis of the why, how, and what that drive the news and the consumers of news, he does touch on "what to do." Zada's brief concluding suggestions for action, understandably perhaps, are mostly geared to those in the media, with some suggestions quite doable and others less so. Unlike the litany of diagnostics and forensics offering no remedy that most publishers continue to launch upon us, he makes the attempt. But, while an interesting read, clearly this is not enough.

Unfortunately, warnings are not remedies—and, in the United States and many other countries, it is in the disinformation land of the suburbs that elections are so often decided. It should be obvious to anyone paying attention that the old claim that the news informs to develop an informed electorate, for example, just isn't true. And, apart from a relatively few notable bright lights in the media, op-eds and cable channel megaphones don't much help.

So, who will offer more than is needed of what really matters? Namely, support for the ongoing fights to sustain freedoms of thought, speech, and association. For a start, this includes putting an even brighter spotlight on the actions needed yesterday to:

* Codify the much talked about guardrails of democracy, to promptly and vigorously prosecute violators.

* Dismantle propaganda everywhere possible.

* Replace the grifters and charlatans who currently are making "news" with what the decent, elected representatives are doing, rather than what they're wrangling about doing.

* Use the undoubted power of the media to creatively develop analytic and critical abilities among all generations.

Before too many naysayers line up, let's remember what the media can do when truly creative individuals have a go. Long-running are some genuine accomplishments of media organizations partnering with initiative-takers, to bring freshness in some areas beyond the news—often with very young audiences, like *Sesame Street, Play School,* and *Blue Peter.*

Who will invent the next new, new thing that enlivens the ongoing fights for freedoms of thought, speech, and association?

December 1, 2021

Pundit Propaganda

Barnum & Bailey clowns, geese, roosters, and donkey
by The Strobridge Litho. Co./Library of Congress (restored, rotated & cropped).
This image is in the Public Domain {{PD-US-expired}}
https://commons.wikimedia.org/wiki/File:Barnum_%26_Bailey_clowns_and_geese2.jpg

Propagandist Pundits play too much with our perception. Will such folks ever appreciate that, if we really do hanker for the current equivalent of ***performing geese, roosters, & a musical donkey,*** we'll find a real circus.

NOT talking here about the so obvious pundits, whom we regrettably notice too much–these are the self-servers, who routinely speak conspiracy lies, or so much that's outrageous, that, if they had a moral compass, or any of the faith that some of them claim, their comments would surely head them hellward. NOR those mentioned recently in an opinion article in the newspaper, which suggested that pundits should own up when they get something wrong, just like the rest of us do, when inevitably in life we make a mistake.

Important as those are to address, more important are pundits who try to put truthful perspective yet fail. And these pundits are important because of their potential! These are the folks who too often fail by being unwitting propagandists, constantly parroting the words and claims of some grifter, charlatan, propagandist, or other pretender–thereby publicizing a pretender's original claims. These prevalent and persistent pundits are particularly dangerous and destructive to democracy.

Ever since the first televised presidential debates in the United States in 1960, we've known that pundits who soon afterwards comment on what public figures say have more power than the original remarks. As mentioned in an earlier blog post, this was already evident as long ago as 1943, when the brilliant pundit Martin Esslin–well before he famously described the theater of the absurd–participated in counter-propaganda radio broadcasts. His role was to immediately analyze Hitler's speeches, and Esslin's analyses–which were unfavorable to the Nazis–were broadcast in German into occupied countries, where people were allowed to listen only to radio broadcasts in German.

Today, we need more pundits who use their own words more, to comment truthfully, positively, and plainly. To do this, many need to stop repeating the language of pretenders. For example, when will people's attraction to alliteration give way to sense? Should be plain as day that, if you keep quoting the audience-tested, much propagated slogan "St** the St***," you're helping the propagandist by spreading bad words (and lies) again, and again, and again, etc. And it should be just fine for moderators on broadcast media or editors in the print media to use different words to challenge this as propaganda. No different than the responsibility to prevent dissemination of libel and slander, and unchecked propaganda is at least as dangerous.

Dear Pundit, if you really must have a slogan to repeat, or a bumper sticker to put up somewhere prominently, how about the alliterative **"Stop the Stupid."** Or, instead of still repeating "no fr**d was found," just dump the negatives—and say what's **Fair** for **Freedom** of thought, speech, and association. It's simple to do when you remember what's at stake.

But perhaps these pundits feel purified by putting a negative in front of their free publicity for some pretender—whom they ironically often decry—then do detailed forensics, reusing the pretender's fantasy verbiage, and repeat the original words and claims endlessly, sometimes putting "not" in front; mistakenly believing that "not" has some power that it actually lacks.

For example, if I said to you "Don't WALK on the grass," likely you'd hear most prominently the verb "walk" and what follows it, even if I'd not capitalized, which equals SHOUTING this verb, or if I'd used "not" instead of the barely noticeable contraction ...*n't*. Have you noticed also that verbs are more powerful in getting our attention than nouns and negatives... or just about any other bit of language. This imperative or instruction form of the verb is especially powerful and attention-getting because it rarely occurs in conversation. This gives added inclination for your brain to totally ignore the negative and hear something more like "Go ahead, you (or y'all) go walk on the grass!!"

Out of habit, or dancing around legalisms, or ignorance, or just being lazy though, people do negate or double-negate comments, all the time. Some even double-negate themselves into insulting followers, as was reported recently.

It really is simple to rephrase or paraphrase, to purify the puerile and pernicious. How about just saying "X & Y have occurred, and Z suggests/ed this remedy..." instead of the usual pattern, "This killer fog that I'm showing you again and again will not go away anytime soon." Maybe cross the street, so-to-speak, to find someone who will offer a remedy to pursue, rather than continuing to provide a platform for some "Desdemona-downer" pretender! Or, for additional thoughts on what language to use, please re-check George Orwell's essay, "Politics and the English Language."

It's not only preference for the positive that prompted this post. Among Jacques Ellul's warnings about propaganda is an alert to what he called social propaganda. This most powerful propaganda drives automatic behavior, triggered from the assumptions and norms wrapped within the context and language that we swim in every day. Even if you're not perturbed about the impact of all these "nots" not-not-negating us into nothingness or worse, media bullhorns that repeat foul fantasies and pretense just perpetuate the mind warp first intended.

Anyway, please consider that a great many people are just plain tired of hearing all the swamp talk of pretenders repeated. Surely, it's time to find a better way to call out the putrid and the puerile? How about perorating the promising? Now there's a prospect!

A pundit is supposed to be, and is often paid to be, well, better—with an opinion to share, with perspective and precision. So, please, can this include putting a stop to promoting drivel?

January 13, 2022

The Back-seat Driver

Passenger Compartment, Rambler Ranch
by CZmarlin Christopher Siemnowicz is licensed under CCA-SA-4.0 International.
https://commons.wikimedia.org/wiki/File:1967_AMC_Ambassador_DPL_convertible_in_Sungold_M etallic_and_tan-gold_interior_at_Rambler_Ranch_7of8.jpg

Did you ever experience in the years before Covid-19, when driving a vehicle with seats fully occupied, the occasional passenger—usually from the back seat—who instructed the best time to brake, or turn, or accelerate, or which route to take?

One of the unexpected benefits of the pandemic is the effective disappearance of this individual from many vehicles, mainly because sane people no longer tend to take weekend drives or carpool with lots of passengers.

Unfortunately, not to be suppressed by anything serious like a pandemic, this impulse to instruct from the back seat has visibly increased in other places.

You might have noticed there seem now to be a very large number of people suddenly qualified in their minds to judge how test kits and vaccines can be magically produced and distributed, how the virus works, what are the effective remedies, what safety protocols should pertain, how hard-done-by they are compared to everyone else, and the list goes on.

Somehow, this infects some media talk show hosts, and program anchors, and reporters, and Mr. or Ms. Interviewee, all of whom—as quickly and uninformed as a back-seat driver—megaphone their snappy instructions or question the efforts of healthcare workers, government, and everyone else, without reference to or any apparent knowledge of realities like production and delivery, or of surges in demand set off by panic.

Perhaps it's unsurprising that healthcare workers in some hospitals are now being issued body armor, yes, Kevlar jackets, etc., etc., as protection from incoming patients who react violently to having their barmy treatment instructions to the healthcare workers denied.

Ignoring the back-seat driver apparently no longer works. What to do? What happened to working together to defeat a common enemy, namely the virus!

Perhaps to paraphrase Pogo, it's time to address the enemy within, who is us?

December 29, 2021

How Anti-social Are Social Media?

Smartphone
by Gerd Altmann licensed under Pixabay.

While legislators and the providers of social media platforms quibble, serious questions continuously emerge about the "social" value or otherwise of social media. How much the social media harm social cohesion is a concern of pundits and analysts, and many others of us. A *New Yorker* article by Gideon Lewis-Kraus on June 3 this year surveys the ongoing tussle over these serious questions.

In developing democracies or for push-back against autocrats, social media allow people to share information and grow group cohesion. Elsewhere, questions are often asked, like whether social media "make people angrier... more... polarized... create political echo chambers... increase... violence... [or] enable foreign governments to increase political dysfunction in the United States and other democracies?"

Or, whether social media leave us "particularly vulnerable to confirmation bias, or the propensity to fix upon evidence that shores up our prior beliefs?" Or, whether "social media might be more of an amplifier of other things going on?"

All good questions deserving better answers. But more simply, I would ask: If social media executives really believe that what they do is so purely a social good, why do so many Silicon Valley parents, who manage many of these companies, ration the amount of time their offspring devote to social media? Can't recall this advice being urged on the rest of us with any consistency by social media executives, their lobbyists, or industry representatives.

Some studies of social media effects are inconclusive, disputed, or ongoing (forever?). Meanwhile, teen suicide, gun violence, and political dysfunction undeniably intersect with social media daily.

Of all the questions mentioned in the *New Yorker* article, perhaps the most important is whether society can really wait around another five or ten years for more literature reviews?

A variety of individuals and organizations keep exploiting social media. This is serious value for the companies providing the platforms, who spend substantially on talented specialists to develop the algorithms and drive up the use of social media—at least, where Western-styled salaries, bonuses, and stock options are paid! But social media entice serious activity by trolls, zealots, and dilettantes too!

Of course, it's the people using social media who are really exploited. In exchange for their time and using a bit of intelligence to acquire some *know-how*, social media users can reach a variety of people for a variety of purposes—while also stimulating considerable dopamine in the brain, to help fulfill the social media companies' main purpose, of getting more people to occupy more time on social media.

Minimally, should society make social media providers abide by requirements equivalent to what govern mass media?

How long will it be before legislators do something about any of these matters, instead of muddling along at buggy speed in a nanosecond world?

Note

Gideon Lewis-Kraus (2022), "How Harmful is Social Media," *The New Yorker,* June 3, https://www.newyorker.com/culture/annals-of-inquiry/we-know-less-about-social-media-than-we-think?

June 16, 2022

What's Real?

Dropcentre Tram, prior to enclosed driver cabin
by unknown author, John Oxley Library, Queensland, Public Domain {{PD-US-expired}}
https://commons.wikimedia.org/wiki/File:BrisbaneDropcentreTram242NewFarmFerryTerminus1925.jpg

As far back as memory, books and bookshelves! Being read to when very young stimulated voracious reading when older. In late childhood, the weekly routine included a Saturday morning tramway ride to the not-so-local public library, which invited further reading interests.

Hours were spent in the library, lost in the stacks of books, including novels, short stories, poetry, and criticism, as well as local and international newspapers, and magazines or journals about whatever held interest at the time—like astronomy, the season's sport, looking after pets, and later, books on history, rhetoric, or propaganda.

The morning spent leafing through titles had to conclude well before the mid-day closing time, to stand in line with everyone else, and hear the librarian quip about each item as it was checked out—to join that week's ration of the most books able to be carried, for the journey home on the rattling tram.

These older trams were called "bone-shakers" for a reason. Each weekday, it was an experience to also travel by tram to school.

Most passengers rushed first to occupy the never large enough, enclosed cabins at each end of the tram. It was the unlucky or the undaunted, who found a location on the middle platform between the cabins—to sit in the open-air on wooden-slat seats or stand hanging on to leather straps overhead—some of us were glad to feel the breeze as the tram picked up speed, others just grudgingly thankful to be underway to some destination. And all of us exposed to the traffic noise and exhaust fumes, the wind, the tropical sun, or rain squalls, in the heat or cold that the seasons brought, for the six-mile journey each way.

Some of the undaunted, while standing and swaying to the curves of the road or jerking with stops and starts along the route had mastered reading newspapers or books one-handed. The more social passengers talked and laughed, strangers as they met, to become firm acquaintances and possibly meet again on later travels.

Through travel experiences never ideal, people were mostly good natured and helpful, looking out for one another—alerting the tram-driver to wait up by pulling the bell cord sharply, when children, or the elderly, or someone unwell, or with larger packages needed extra time boarding or alighting. Strangers looked out for strangers, with some sense of care and safety enveloping everyone.

Maybe you have memories that are different yet feel basically similar to times like this. Whether realities experienced are long past or recent, memories are a touchstone to what's real—but any day in our experience will be very different from a great many stories in the daily news.

Connotations and the texture of words matter to capture what's real. We know that understanding these qualities in words is learned gradually over time, through listening or reading with care and attention to the nuance of words. For anyone in the business of news, this is well understood.

Yet how damaging is the intoxication to write news stories that repeat verbatim so many delusions of the outrageous, the trivial, and the bizarre—repeating ad nauseam the hyperbolic words of media releases. Today's media inherited from the continuously declining tabloid press the reward of urgency and conflict-based stories, or "balancing" one set of opinions against another.

Some gatekeepers in the mainstream media and journalists are taking responsibility to pursue a more constructive approach to deliver news. For this "constructive journalism," the media only report comment from politicians that is evidence-based and can be evaluated by "pegging their words back to reality" (Pomerantsev, p. 239).

August 12, 2022

Polls

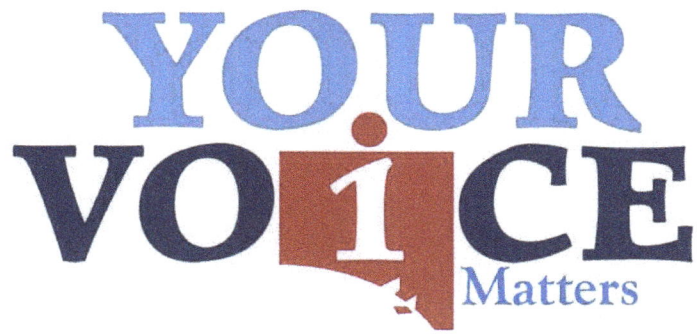

Your voice matters party material
Your Voice Matters party logo is licensed under CCA-SA 3.O Unported.
https://commons.wikimedia.org/wiki/File:Your_voice_Matters_logo.jpg

Masquerading as breaking news this morning was the "bombshell insight" that claims 29% of us believe the United States is headed in the right direction. This gem of intelligence is hauled out periodically, often on a slow news day, or when a pundit wants to probe a pet peeve.

As an all-purpose stimulant of meaningless commentary, a new twist this morning was the reframing as a positive statement. Usually, we'd be told 71% of us believe we're headed in the wrong direction. Maybe that was considered too tough to take with the morning coffee.

This "news" again occupied the serious conversation of ordinarily sensible pundits on a cable TV station for ages today, as they discussed the shocking wisdom, from an unimaginable variety of approaches. Not mentioned were the questionable ambiguities in the question to secure this statistic. We're no wiser about what anyone believes is "right" or "wrong," or even what these terms mean.

Other than feeling gloomy or launching speculations of one's own, what's anyone to think, say, or do about what? It's barely useful even as an indicator of sentiment because of inherent ambiguities. Probably the only certainty from this poll is that it helps to shore up existing prejudices.

Regrettably, even missing now from the media presentation of poll results most of the time are the sample size, margin of error, and date the poll was conducted. But with this poll so flawed, contextual facts don't really matter.

The hazards of opinion polling affect us all in too many ways to outline briefly. But putting aside any feeling that polls are facts is a safe bet. In his unique way, Peter Cook shared a not-so-gentle warning about the potential hazard of polls as long ago as 1970–in the film, *The Rise and Rise of Michael Rimmer* (David Paradine Productions).

What matters in this silly season of electioneering is to be wary of polls–along with making a plan to vote in the one important poll, when you can.

Note

David Paradine Productions/Kevin Billington (1970), *The Rise and Rise of Michael Rimmer*, https://www.youtube.com/watch?v=fPE-vddZ-aA

October 12, 2022

Propaganda

Not Propaganda?

The meeting of day and night in a mountain valley with invisible pink unicorn
By Vian, modified by Robin A Smile, is licensed under CCA-SA 4.0 International.
https://commons.wikimedia.org/wiki/File:The_meeting_of_day_and_night_in_a_mountain_valley_wit
h_invisible_pink_unicorn.jpg

Most attributed to the philosopher Immanuel Kant are rules for happiness: something to do; someone to love; and something to hope for.

It's helpful to keep these rules nearby when wading into Peter Pomerantsev's Adventures in the War Against Reality, which is the subtitle of his book *This Is NOT Propaganda*. The front cover to my copy of the book projects optimism, with its rainbow, unicorn, and some praise in words listed from reviews. Best be prepared though that, intriguing and lively as the narration is, this well-written scrutiny of 21st century agents of "doublespeak" probably won't cheer you up–it details the activities of people whom George Orwell had warned us to expect, back in 1949.

The author provides an update that such "doublespeak" agents are now very real, and very many–to an extent that most of our nearest friends, family, and neighbors might prefer not to know. And these characters, whose stories he tells, seem committed to "do something" day-and-night to make the world a lesser place. They are preoccupied with Kant's first rule. If they'd ever heard of his other rules, their concern would be solely from the point of view of narcissism.

Too much like the fictional folks of a South-East Asian bot farm that was featured in the television series, *The Bureau*, the real people in this book mostly display immorality of the amoral. The book starts with a well-written narrative of some earlier times [spoiler detail averted], as context for the even more disturbing recent past and the present. Both the early narrative and the outlines of more recent times are chilling insight into the post-fact world that propagandists continue to create, which they'd like us all to live in.

So, yes, as yet-another warning, the book lives up to the effusive claim of the reviewers. It is "frightening." Additionally, since this book was written, our real-life challenges are larger–even medical groups now feel obliged to send messages they call "unprecedented," politely asking their patients to be nice–as well as warning that rude communication, unreasonable demands of medical staff, inappropriate language, and making threats will not be tolerated.

We're well along the path of the unacceptable in society when abuse against healthcare workers from patients has reached such a level that it stimulates this request. This is just one of the signals that the long-gestated plans of autocrats, who continue to refine and execute many of the systems of propaganda that contribute polarization and dysfunction throughout the world, are reaching totally unacceptable levels of penetration.

Where are the counter-discussions and actions that might bring improvement to the mess made by propagandists and some other forces exploiting democracy? In the last 27 pages of the book, the author of *This is NOT Propaganda* provides a few glimmers of hope along the lines of Kant's third rule.

Might we hope that journalism schools or, increasingly, practicing journalists will devote some considerable effort to the "constructive news" practices that he mentions? This is an approach that has been around for a while. Instead of "merely 'balancing' one set of opinions against another... [the constructive news approach tries] ...to find practical solutions to the challenges which face its audience, forcing politicians to make evidence-based proposals, which one could then evaluate over time, pegging their words back to reality..." (Pomerantsev, p. 239)

But, to counter the mono-thinking and certainty claims of autocrats, much more is also needed. We face one of the most critical periods of history, in which, more than ever, vigorous efforts are needed to offset propagandists.

Hats off to the ongoing efforts in education to illuminate propaganda by developing the ability in next generations to criticize what's going on, and hopefully take actions needed to do better by everyone. We all owe an enormous debt to decades-long efforts of insightful educationalists—too many to list here.

Of special note are Randal Marlin, whose *Propaganda and the Ethics of Persuasion* remains such a valued classic, and Garth S. Jowett/Victoria O'Donnell, whose thorough text *Propaganda & Persuasion* is soon going to its eighth edition. Additionally, thanks go to Nancy Snow for her many contributions, including her highlighting the role of public diplomacy, as well as to J. Michael Sproule's scholarly clarity on various facets of propaganda, while recommending, as he might say, the pleasures of toil in the vineyards of propaganda.

Continuing efforts are important to sustain understandings beyond such key efforts as the Institute of Propaganda Analysis, founded in 1937 by Edward A. Filene and Clyde R. Miller, as well as the insightful landmark *Propaganda,* published by Jacques Ellul in 1962.

Once you've read *This is NOT Propaganda,* or other warnings concerning the propaganda morass surrounding us all, the question remains, beyond the diagnoses and warnings, what more will you do to help offset these propagandists, who continue to white-ant both our reality and democracy?!

July 25, 2022

Silly Season

Charlie Chaplin (with "double cross" emblem)
from film trailer screenshot, *The Great Dictator*. This image is in the Public Domain.
https://commons.wikimedia.org/wiki/File:Dictator_charlie2.jpg

Thanks to George Orwell's short essay published in 1946, "Politics and the English Language," we can be more alert to public figures using words to obscure or deliberately hide realities.

The eminent British linguist David Crystal, in his 2016 Orwell Lecture to the Emirates Festival of Literature, named Orwell's essay as "one of the most important articles on the language to come out of the 20th century." Yet, together with the many further warnings of the French philosopher, Jacques Ellul and others delineating propaganda processes for us, these combined efforts are clearly not enough to counteract the emergence of added generations of the ideological offspring of Joseph Goebbels or Leni Riefenstahl.

Some robust educational preparations for life are sustained in the United States and other countries. Evidence of this is the remarkably sustained public communication efforts of students from Florida's Parkland High School, following the shootings there in February 2018.

Unfortunately, there is also ample indication that too few people are prepared for the silly season now upon the United States.

An indication of this is a not-so-recent video that's resurfaced, showing the ABC network conducting street-interviews of youths, who are asked to name countries on a map of the world, with no success. What hope then to navigate obscure or deceptive election rhetoric?

Anything can happen as a nation enters the final months of an election.

What's predictable is that "talking points" to "message" us will increase. With each passing day these will sound more alike. For sure, there will be some public figures and pundits still frozen in talking about the "right message" and message sending. They should find a time-machine and take themselves back to the meetings of telephone engineers in the 1940's, when this concept of communication was popularized (and later challenged). C'mon, that was almost 80 years ago, folks.

In our personal lives, we accept that the ingredients that make life worthwhile are trust, common understanding, and commitment to do what truly benefits people, so why should politicians' public talk be judged at any lesser standard?

Do we really have to go back 2,400 years or more to the ancient Chinese philosopher, Lao-Tzu to find the wisdom that "a leader is best when people barely know [she or] he exists"? Wouldn't that be refreshing? More recently, other thoughtful folks like Warren Bennis and Lee Thayer have added that a true leader:

* **Helps** focus a desired state of affairs.

* Asks the right questions to **help** people address challenges.

* **Helps** translate solutions into practice.

It is significant that the leader's duty to help is in every line. It's time to expect leaders to take only actions that help people. This is the test of authenticity that's needed now.

Meantime, in preparation for the drivel about to be spewed forth, I'd urge you to get a copy of the second edition of Randal Marlin's *Propaganda and the Ethics of Persuasion,* Peterborough, ON: Broadview Press, 2013. If you'd like a detailed review, before parting with about $33 on Amazon or elsewhere, google the excellent review by Gary James Jason at California State University.

Despite Jason's final recommendation that the book should be accessible to any serious scholar of propaganda and persuasion, it's actually a straightforward preparation for any of us.

Randal Marlin puts succinctly that:
"PROPAGANDA = The organized attempt through communication to affect belief or action or inculcate attitudes in a large audience in ways that circumvent or suppress an individual's adequately informed, rational, reflective judgment." (Marlin, p. 12)

Not hard to understand. With this very useful definition, quibbles about whether or not all propaganda is harmful get swept away. All propaganda is bad. This is not just my view, but was earlier implied by Jacques Ellul, who pointed out that "to be effective, propaganda must constantly short-circuit all thought and decision" (Ellul, p. 27). The light at the end of the tunnel we're in is that Ellul also noted that propaganda ceased where simple dialogue begins.

The current public "exchanges" about the US Postal Service have special value in the United States. Curtailing this beloved US institution is a loser for such advocates. The limitations on propaganda that Ellul outlined (p. 295-6) are a warning to propagandists and a clue for ways to counter propagandists:

1. Don't mess with people's pre-existing attitudes–propaganda cannot move except within the framework of these attitudes, which it can modify only very slowly (certainly not in the time frame of the final stages of an election).

2. Although propaganda might sometimes overcome general trends of society, the sociological/cultural factors in which people act have an absolute limit. So, in a nation committed to democracy, proselytizing for a monarchy is a loser–instead, tyrants try to claim they are democratic, which counterattacks need to focus vigorously on unmasking.

3. The propagandist is limited by people's need for consonance with facts; so, the counterattack is to reassert and convince people of the solidity of a fact that is right! Propaganda of ideas does not exist. Even "Goebbels changed his propaganda after Stalingrad, because it was impossible to transform that debacle into victory," said Ellul.

Among many other good qualities of Marlin's book are his explanatory list of the common fallacies of reason, in one of the best summaries I've seen, AND similar provided by Eleanor MacLean of the known and less well known examples of how language can be used to manipulate an audience.

It's time to get ready, get personal with email and mutually supportive action, and be prepared to listen up. Slogans matter less in elections than we might think, but this might be time to remember that the 1957 election slogan in Britain "Never had it so good" was turned back, by the opponents' response **"Never been had so good."**

That's the spirit needed now. Going forward, especially in coming weeks, we'll see whether candor of actions matches public talk.

August 23, 2020

Imagine

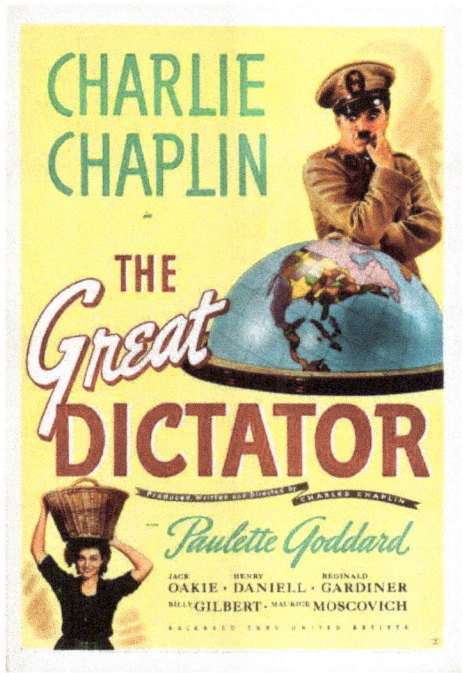

The Great Dictator (1940) poster
by United Artists, retouched by Brandt Luke Zorn.
This image is in the Public Domain {{PD-US-not renewed}}
https://commons.wikimedia.org/wiki/File:The_Great_Dictator_(1940)_poster.jpg

Alexander Hamilton warned in *The Federalist, Number 8:*

> ...the continual effort and alarm attendant on a state of continual danger will compel nations the most attached to liberty to resort for repose and security to institutions which have a tendency to destroy their civil and political rights. To be more safe, they at length become willing to run the risk of being less free.

Although Hamilton was commenting on the effect of chaos from war upon a nation, this is also the clue to why a propagandist stimulates continual chaos.

The foremost writer on this subject, the French philosopher, Jacques Ellul warned long ago that the propagandist needed:

> ...continuous agitation... [to] create a climate first, and then prevent the individual from noticing a particular propaganda operation in contrast to ordinary daily events. (Ellul, p. 20)

Almost 40 years ago in an address to a Royal Society gathering focused on public information, I drew on Ellul to urge awareness about how we are all propagandized. As the most educated, intelligent people in the community, my audience was the most propagandized, because they:

(1) Absorbed the largest amount of second-hand information.
(2) Felt some compulsion to have an opinion.
(3) Considered themselves capable of "judging." (Ellul, p. vi)

When our world view is so dominated with one leader's name, with the media conducting endless analysis and regurgitation of that leader's statements or views, **we are being abused.**

It's time to imagine a better way.

One lesson from the Covid-19 experience is that social distancing works—by analogy, we should separate ourselves from a propagandist's messages and the "busy work" of reacting to them. You can keep the virus known as propaganda at a distance too.

The actor Peter Finch, in the film *Network*, modeled a first step along these lines when he declared:

"I'm as mad as hell, and I'm not going to take this anymore..."

Otherwise, as Ellul also warned, each of us can become:

> ...suited to a totalitarian society, ...not at ease except when integrated in the mass, ...reject[ing] critical judgment, choices and differentiations because... [we] ...cling to clear certainties... assimilated into uniform groups and want it that way. (Ellul, p. 256)

Internationally, peaceful protests have shown one way to divert such a dismal future. **It's time to imagine** (among the many choices) how you will deploy your talents in 2020.

Is there nothing you can do? What will you do?

Note

Metro-Goldwyn-Mayer/Sidney Lumet (1976), "I'm as mad as hell, and I'm not going to take this anymore! Speech from *Network*," https://www.youtube.com/watch?v=ZwMVMbmQBug

June 14, 2020

It's Time for Plain Talk

George Orwell Statue – BBC Broadcasting House
The wall behind is inscribed with the words
"If liberty means anything at all,
it means the right to tell people
what they do not want to hear,"
from his proposed preface to Animal Farm.
by Matt Brown, MattFromLondon is licensed under CCA 2.0 Generic.
https://commons.wikimedia.org/wiki/File:George_Orwell_statue_-_BBC_London_(38562767202).jpg

Augustus Saint-Gaudens, an American sculptor of the Beaux-Arts generation, once remarked that "...it's the way a thing's done that makes it right or wrong."

When it comes to public talk, I believe we're long overdue for some plain talk about what we should accept as right. Too many public conversations now (obviously tweets too) are just, well, **"wrong," "off,"**

"cringeworthy," "inappropriate," or **"unacceptable."** Take your pick or waste more energy on expletives and likely you'll be closest to right.

Here, I'm not referring to comments like someone describing an opponent as *"simply a shiver looking for a spine to run up."* With variants tracing back to at least 1966, the endurance of this artful and possibly apt jibe is welcome to everyone except the latest target of the quip.

Doublethink

No, what we need is plain talk about what George Orwell named "doublethink," and its close relative "doubletalk."

This is "a process of indoctrination whereby the subject is expected to accept as true that which is clearly false, or to simultaneously accept two mutually contradictory beliefs as correct, often in contravention to one's own memories or sense of reality." (Wikipedia)

In his day and way, Sir Winston Churchill wrote on this:

> A modern dictator with the resources of science at his disposal can easily lead the public on from day to day, destroying all persistency of thought and aim, so that memory is blurred by the multiplicity of daily news and judgment baffled by its perversion. (Churchill, p. 490)

Why then are there not more of us carrying out Orwell's urging to jeer "...loudly enough, [to] send some ...lump of verbal refuse ...into the dustbin where it belongs."

Fact-checks

For example, there are good reasons to believe that fact-checking, as it's mostly done, is a fool's fantasy. Firstly, once prejudices are established and continuously reinforced, including through the mail, media or social media, the "tribe" will not believe any criticism from any source about a tribal leader's corruption or malfeasance.

Further, it is clear so-called fact-checking, or otherwise restating a message by repeating it (even in the negative), just reinforces the original propaganda. Both the believers and the undecided will focus on the original false message and ignore that little word "not" or other negation that the fact checker inserts. The negative is as invisible as the bicyclists whom car drivers genuinely don't see on the road.

To Counter

There are right ways to counter the emergence of the ideological offspring of Joseph Goebbels or Leni Riefenstahl. These include:

1. Ignore any verbal refuse designed to distract, deny or delay—by all means, counter with the truth but, please, oh please, stop repeating the words of the original—you're just being a megaphone for what you oppose.

2. Listen up, friends in the media, there's not much that a bad actor fears more than being ignored—at the very least, **stop** using or repeating a bad actor's name: **stop** repeating direct quotes in the lower thirds of the television screen; and **stop** showing "B-Roll" of a bad actor, instead of paraphrasing any comments, if needed at all.

3. Encourage leaks of sensitive information that expose lies and fraud.

4. Reverse any serious lie right back onto the liar—use words much like the graffiti artist sprays a mustache on a propaganda poster.

5. Exponentially grow networks of person to person communications, especially through personalized emails and tweets.

Finally, if you believe you can win doing it right, and you put in the effort to communicate vigorously and well, you will win.

June 25, 2020

What to Do

Jacques Ellul
by Jan van Boeckel, ReRun Productions (cropped)
is licensed under CCA-BY-SA-4.0 International.
https://upload.wikimedia.org/wikipedia/commons/c/c8/Jacques_Ellul_crop.jpg

A Gary Larson cartoon that a friend recently shared illustrates, by analogy, some of the dilemma the United States faces tackling domestic terrorism.

In the cartoon, four pampered pooches are standing together in a green field. They are looking toward the edge of trees or woods on the left, and behind them is a pull-cart, with one dog in harness to the cart. The cart is stacked with a few large books that are labeled *Domestication*. The pooches are well-groomed and relaxed, with the lead dog standing on hind legs to read aloud from a large open book, also labeled *Domestication*. This optimistic pooch directs the reading from the book toward the woods, where a wolf-pack glares back at the well-mannered dogs, the wolves fixed in their gaze upon the dogs, and poised for attack, clearly anticipating lunch.

Putting aside the visual exaggeration the cartoonist uses to create the comic, the dilemma remains that "we the people" (also known as "lunch") lack a playbook to handle effectively much less to *domesticate* propagandists–who ruthlessly wield propaganda as a weapon. The propagandists' onslaughts of delusional, destabilizing, distracting, and frequently disgustingly offensive words and images help distort the attention, actions, beliefs, and social values of each of us and our fellow citizens.

And wouldn't it be a good thought to have some ways to address the real and present threats of domestic terrorists committed to destroying democracy? Especially since mainstream and social media so frequently megaphone the propagandist rants and outrage, thereby assisting the efforts to white-ant democracy!

It was more than two decades ago, on the day after 9/11 with a dozen bomb alerts in just one day, that my wife wisely and sadly said this would change the country forever. Soon afterwards, to handle the threat from foreign terrorism, domestically we all built practices to lessen risk.

But it was two years ago that a neighbor wanted to *help fight the coup*. This then-odd comment was stimulated by a domestic wannabe leader's using such words repeatedly in mailings to the neighbor and so many others. I knew then we were at the beginning of a very different reality.

Domestic terrorists have used age-old emotional appeals, such as fear of "others" or an array of desires... for recognition, for virility, for accomplishment or for belonging, to strengthen connection with adherents and to acquire new followers for the propagandist's worldview.

Unfortunately, as a society, we are well primed to tolerate and respond to propaganda processes, thanks to generations of political and commercial propagandists working us over. For example, perhaps we think of rumor and fashion as two very different realities that we live with. Yet they are very similar in how potently and quickly each spread and stimulate automatic responses. As Jacques Ellul pointed out, rumor and fashion are forms of propaganda; it's just that for self-interest and in the interests of commerce, we allow fashion a more friendly connotation.

Fads of fashion are spread by *ad populum* appeals, advancing a herd-mentality, especially when supported by advertising campaigns. Just one odd example was the now, little-seen yo-yo. This toy, for anyone not familiar with it, consists of small discs joined by an axle spinning at the end of a piece of string, and was featured as far back as 440 BC on a Greek vase. The toy's popularity has waxed and waned over the centuries. From the 1960s, the yo-yo saw a comeback campaign, with a series of television advertisements. It was also used to help sell otherwise unrelated products, as yo-yo dexterous performers toured the world's schools and fairgrounds; and, by the way, promoted products.

These folks displayed skill we wanted to emulate, by delivering amazing tricks with these spinning disks at the end of a piece of string, from the basic "walk-the-dog," which every self-respecting schoolkid might master, to "around-the-world," "rock-the-cradle," and other more elaborate tricks that only the truly competent could tackle after much practice.

All this seemed fairly harmless. It was certainly less immediately dangerous than the physical harm dealt out in some enduringly fashionable contact sports. Yes, fashion is quite the driver of a range of behaviors, including the banal, like hula-hoops, emoji, and the assigning of "likes."

The problem that occurs for "we the people" is when the propagandist, whether commercial or cult-promoting, can find from among all the possible responses that we might make, a relational response that connects us to the propagandist's objective. In other words, we, the propagandized give ourselves over to automatic response to what's said by the propagandist about what's going on around us.

Or, putting this into pulp-talk, when anyone enters that zombie-zone, even someone silently scorning the propagandist or related conspiracy theorists or partisan politicians and pundits, that person becomes a participant in the propagandist's play. A more engaged level in the zombie-zone is when you spend energy on criticizing the propagandist. This usually requires repeating and therefore promoting the propagandist's name and some foolishness or dogma, while making the criticism. Maybe more importantly, it also means you're wasting your time in the propagandist's alternative reality, taking you away from real reality.

In his comprehensive and nuanced book *Propaganda,* Jacques Elull concluded by illustrating where propaganda could fail. He implied ways to mount counterattacks, to diminish the impact of propaganda, as I've outlined in other blog posts. The strategies he described are potent, as are the recommendations more recently in the work of Randal Marlin, so well-grounded in the wisdom of both Ellul and Orwell. All these writers have serious value in these times. Each helps to build further principles and techniques for the practical dismantling of propaganda.

It's good that many school curricula have increasingly included ways to identify and counter propaganda techniques. Many incorporate simple approaches for dismissing the inane emotional fallacies of much advertising; but more and broader efforts are needed.

For example, further strengthening is needed more widely of efforts to teach writing through a problem-solving approach, to advance writing as thinking. For some insights on this, do take a look at former colleague, Roslyn Petelin's interview of Professor David Crystal in 2014 (on YouTube). Crystal raised concern about the absence of grammar from most writing classrooms from the 1960s up until the 1990s, which, as Petelin pointed out, Professor John Frow called "a calamity." Hard to figure how one's supposed to write thoughtfully without a workable knowledge of grammar. Whatever fashion drove this impulse might periodically still need dismantling.

In relation to the domestic terrorists in the United States, it's a reasonable start to keep calling terrorists what they are and to keep calling out lies or "the big lie," while prosecuting illegal behaviors. We do also need to get beyond these first stages and address the systemic challenges though.

What will we do to -

* Enhance feelings of belonging in civil society among the propagandist's targets?

* Defuse the impact of rumor that occurs through social media and otherwise, which gains power, as Ellul noted, "...the more the objective fact loses importance and the more the rumor is believed by the multitudes who adhere to it"? (pp. 293-4)

* Nurture a variety of viewpoints through stepped-up "conversation and dialogue... [that is] open" as Ellul urged–to sharpen doubts about formulaic comments, and lessen the likelihood of responding to a propagandist? (p. 300)

* Intercept the spontaneous responses to a propagandist, before any of these become learned responses connected to the propagandist's objective? (p. 301)

Brainwashing seeks to weaken independent thought and absorb the individual into the mass. Ellul pointed out that propaganda more broadly also aims to eliminate individualizing factors. He warned that: "At the moment when the attitudes learned by propaganda begin to prevail over... [what is] ...second nature, they become collective, and the propagandist who has taught them can then calculate more easily what a given stimulus will elicit from them (p. 302)."

Our better future will be found through the vigor of our strengthening individual thought.

February 24, 2021

Funny That...

Alien abduction
by Travis Walton (reconstitution). This image is in the Public Domain.
https://commons.wikimedia.org/wiki/File:Walton(reconstitution).png

Did you know that long-time Monty Python fan and former member of The Beatles, George Harrison mortgaged his quite expensive house to fund the production of the movie, *Life of Brian*? If you did, you might have what it takes to win some counter-propaganda efforts, since I just learned this from a vintage documentary. You had the advantage to be first (probably way before me, anyway).

Continuing the theme, of all people, Woody Allen not just humorously alerted us to the important quality of being first. He pointed out that the world should not be so preoccupied with any invaders from outer space having a technology that's many years ahead of ours. He claimed it was not advanced technologies supported by plans for world domination that will win. He worried about the invading force that was equipped to be anywhere even fifteen minutes ahead of us.

It's the same with propaganda. Being first wins, especially followed up with high repetition.

Which is why the bad actor (or just about any savvy politician) likes to give his or her version of bad news first, or at least be quickest to reframe the story after the breaking news. Of course, a bad actor who has lots of bad news sometimes takes a little longer to weigh up which bad news has enough traction to need response. This delay gives quick-off-the mark counterpropaganda the opportunity for added advantage.

Which is also why, during my brushes with politics, breakfast brainstorming sessions to counter anticipated propaganda was so often the advantage that won airtime.

Because being first applies to counterpropaganda too. Enough with all the micro-analyses. Just get ahead of the game–fifteen minutes ahead, at least.

Some media interviewers are very effective at walking bad actors into disclosing themselves. But those media people who have long-winded, polite interviews about or with crooks will never really succeed in keeping them accountable. And you don't need nuanced understanding of someone picking your pocket, you need to stop them.

If you feel this might not be democratic, I'd counter that you're reasserting simple dialogue–which is kryptonite to propaganda with its sole purpose of mindless obedience as well as to the bad actor behind it.

No time now to be writing instruction books and action plans either. Just counterpropaganda ahead of the continuous stream of drivel is what matters now.

September 13, 2020

It's the PROPAGANDA, Stu***

Traditional three-legged chair, Museum of Pedagogy, Belgrade
by Milica Buha is licensed under CCA-BY-SA-4.0 International.
https://commons.wikimedia.org/wiki/File:Tronozac_(three-legged_chair).jpg

Today's message is to the media (and all of us, really). Here are the delusions:

"I get personal tweets..." –along with some multi-million others!

"The stock market is up..."–this 47% of the population now own the national debt pumped into the financial markets.

"THEY will take it all off you..."–the biggest fear of all...

In the old days, when my father was selling milking separators to dairy farmers, the farmer had a three-legged chair to sit on while milking the cows. It had three legs, so it stood firmly on any uneven ground.

Three propaganda assaults still work to milk us, apparently. With what flows from each assault spreading like a virus, or to mix figurative language more, like Triffids (could be worth looking this one up). The propagandist counts on your engagement with one or other of the viral "news" flows, while propagating another... and throwing at you the fertilizers of outrage, exaggeration, and repetition. If you're tantalized by such tractor-beams, as pictured in my previous blog, shame on you.

For counterpropaganda, three-legged chairs work too. How about:

1. IGNORE manufactured outrages.
2. Trumpet reality.
3. Advance and frequently repeat what matters to people: **health, shelter, food, safety,** and **freedom.**

Out of these five life positives, surely you can pick three to focus on. At the very least, you'll be in touch with reality and, who knows, when you talk with someone else about what's real, you might help someone else live a little better.

If this is starting to sound like a message with Dick and Dora in a grade-school reading class, it is. You see, I'm willing to IGNORE another successful propagandist who made millions telling you to always flatter your audience. The propagandist knows you will obsess about lies, hyperbole, and insecurities. Don't let it keep happening–it's up to you.

Fact is that the jig is up. Just tell the truth, without quixotically tilting at the propagandist's fantasies. Simple, direct truth hurts the propagandist. Of course, you have to keep choosing what really matters to "we, the people"–see "3" above.

Who has the smarts and discipline to build a new three-legged chair?

September 15, 2020

Certainty Claims

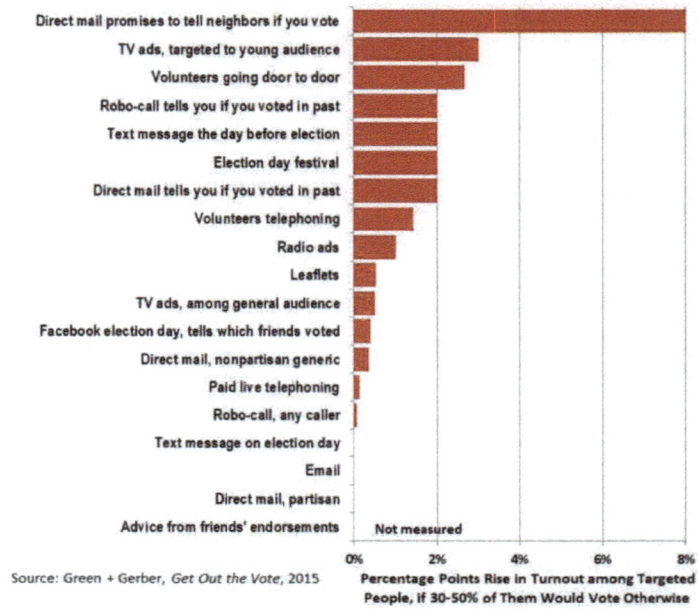

Comparison of different methods to raise voter turnout
GOTV by Numbersinstitute is licensed under CCA-SA 4.0 International.
https://commons.wikimedia.org/wiki/File:GOTV.png

As we re-enter the "silly seasons" of electioneering, in the United States, France, Australia, and elsewhere, it's timely to look afresh at propaganda claims and processes. Not that this or that propagandist's statement or action now is very different, or especially more damaging than the propaganda processes we let wash over us every day–it's just the stakes are even greater. Since a good result in an election can also blunt some effects of propaganda, how we approach an election brings the opportunity to look afresh at what's going on with propagandists–if only to reconsider ways to raise the voter turnout of anyone who believes in democracy.

Often, as an election approaches, the foreboding will be of a Groundhog Day experience–as we anticipate even more intense shouting by the anti-democracy mob, any of whom might live next door. Unfortunately, the United States and some other democracies have a too large crop of shouting wannabes, whose copy-cat tradition is to speak of carnage and how they're so hardly done by–especially by the media–and, with a zealot's energy, will set about attacking others and claim that all will certainly "be best" by reviving some mythical glories of the past–which never include a capacity for laughter or any humor.

And those candidates along with some elected representatives seem to mistakenly believe that they're born to rule. They keep popping up. Their public communication is strikingly similar in its dual focus on themselves and on being "anti-" the values of civil society–especially democratic values. Commonly, they promise certainties, rather than choices. The certainty claims conveniently ignore that, especially from the early to the later stages of an election, many of us would like to have some real choice–including among quality candidates for public office.

Who are propagandists is usually what's most certain–when you know what to look for. Sometimes these propagandists pay lip service to democratic values, but mostly just "scream for the camera," as one Congressional representative astutely described some colleagues from his own party recently. The anti-democratic language of propagandists is preoccupied with at-least-mild exaggeration, or more often hyperbole–to capture the attention of a journalist or a camera.

Mostly, a propagandist is caught up with self-advancement–by any means, at the expense of anyone else–routinely using a high proportion of content words which have unclear referents, along with lots of function words like factive verbs and non-referential adverbs.

It feels strange that the United States government in recent months has done so well, by using declassified intelligence, to anticipate and deal effective blows to blunt the propaganda of a foreign aggressor–yet we the people seem comfortable with domestic propaganda. Why is it that the horrors of lies told by another country are deplorable, while local propaganda is willingly accepted in daily living?

A great amount of electoral and everyday propaganda ironically is from domestic terrorists and their foreign collaborators—mostly focused on the character assassination of opponents, sometimes persistently for many years, during endless fundraising and other mailings or using gossip chains. With the targeting of audiences dictated by some very expensive and ongoing socio-psychographic mapping and "messaging" rules, continuous propaganda is directed at party faithful and potential swing voters throughout the country. Yes, anyone else is as irrelevant as any non-person—who, just like any stateless individual in a foreign conflict, will be characterized as "not us" (Snyder)—with eerily bad outcomes expected to flow from all the "anti-" drivel.

Regrettably, by the time we bother to scrutinize propaganda, much of its damage is already done—with the greatest damage not much talked about, namely how **propaganda over time white-ants personal and social values, changing where we put attention, energy, and action.** As Jacques Ellul warned, for propaganda to succeed the propagandist must control free thought.

What most empowers a propagandist are reactions. So, it surely is time to take a pause, instead of taking to Twitter, or devising that media exposé of this or that propagandist, or feeling threatened, or otherwise responding to the impulses of fight or flight when our raw nerves are touched off by a propagandist's emotive nonsense.

It's often safest and best to assume that a propagandist is weird, driven to develop extraordinary skills in self-preservation from probably a very early age, by a distorted commitment to being right and winning—at everything, by whatever means—including as an adult through remarkably protracted gaming of the legal system. All the lies, distortions, and dodges are tactics to prove to anyone who'll react that the propagandist is right and a winner, at your cost.

Of course, as noted in earlier blog posts, pundits frequently do additional damage with so-called fact-checking or other clumsy analyses, disseminating a lie much more widely than the propagandist could manage. And those nauseating excuses by the pundits on mainstream or social media that "only show you this, so you know what's going on" just repeat and magnify the propagandist's insult and abuse.

So, what are we to do?

1. We could stop being obsessed with the aberrant behavior of the propagandist. It's better to pay attention to asserting, with truthful, lawful, and just speech, the practical initiatives that build and strengthen the values of Western civilization–like justice, temperance, courage, and wisdom, or even at a local level what's accomplished, for example, improving health services, roads, or bridges etc. It's better to ensure accountability, soon and well, of anyone whose "anti-" behavior violates existing law. And it's more than time to find ways to "clean house" of any unqualified "anti-democratic" administrators and judiciary.

2. We could be skeptical of glib commentary, especially when it's just too neat, outlandish, or sounds too good to be true–these con-artists learned from wolves to dress up as sheep, and will bleat way too loudly, way above their weight. It's important to scrutinize a propagandist's actions or claims, to assess what impact these will make on freedoms of thought, speech, or association, and on the common good of people. This scrutiny and any needed actions in response are necessary for democracy to thrive.

3. We could stand up to the now too common virulent variety of propaganda that abuses or threatens your personality or safety–we no longer tolerate such abuse in domestic or workplace settings. It's hard to figure why that behavior is tolerated, and not called out more at school board meetings and other community gatherings, much less in legislatures or at the supermarket checkout–with persistent "anti-" claims about masks or vaccination, for example, still popping up in unexpected places. Some chairpersons and individuals are objecting to and successfully

moderating that behavior, which requires some verbal whack-a-mole skills.

4. For all the propaganda processes and puffing and stuffing and hot words, it's best to look away from the propagandist promises of certainty for what's authentic and achievable.

The propagandist thrives by receiving attention. In the time that any of us is objecting to the latest outlandish outrage, our own comments will often exponentially assist the viral spread of drivel. At the same time, the propagandist will launch more vitriol to suck(er) more people into weird obsession with delusions of the propagandist's invention.

And all those appeals to people's fears, grievances, greed, hates, wanting to belong, or other emotions are just a means to an end for propagandists—along with their lies, denials, delays, distortions, and disruptions that are megaphoned and further magnified unwittingly or willingly by mainstream and social media.

Unfortunately, as much as one believes in democratic debate, this is not a belief shared by any propagandist. Ordinarily a propagandist's comments are couched as "not-for-debate." And it's tough to debate the self-absorbed. It's mostly pointless to argue or 'splain propagandist comments, other than as a counterpoint to reassert or demonstrate democratic values of civil society.

The propagandist sees nothing but "selling" us on anything that advances the wannabe goals of the propagandist. Which also makes efforts to describe a propagandist's ideological commitment about as meaningful or useful as trying to label the Wizard of Oz. The better efforts will be to raise voter turnout.

April 22, 2022

The Cons

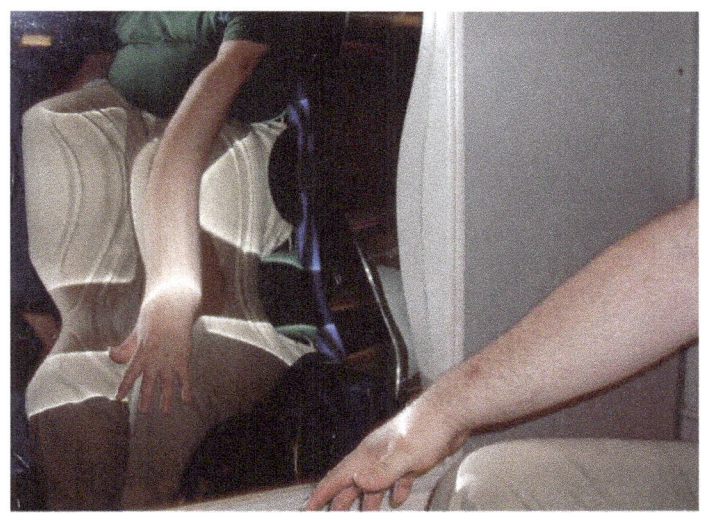

Wirkung eines Zerrspeigels
by –Xocolatl. This image is in the Public Domain.
https://commons.wikimedia.org/wiki/File:Zerrspiegel.jpg

It's all done with mirrors. A once-famous columnist for a still-famous newspaper probably had this saying in mind when he speculated more than half a century ago about writing the ideal all-purpose political speech—by appealing to anyone who's committed to any side of just about any issue. He went further to write, tongue-in-cheek I hope, his own best effort toward earning "the supreme accolade: 'Nobody can quarrel with that.'"

It's worrisome that he was also a presidential speechwriter for five years in an administration not noted for covering itself in glory. While the columnist's name might not matter anymore, the sentiment does, whether or not the original motivation was mainly comic. The columnist proffered that the way to earn the "supreme accolade" was to craft words that permitted political candidates "to take firm stands on all sides of every issue." What's happened to political language since elevates this cheeky comment to seriously worrisome.

We all long ago let ourselves get used to propaganda washing over us every day in every way. Perhaps it's not surprising that, for too many decades in this country, some generators of political language have borrowed and "improved" the techniques that Madison Avenue found sufficiently useful to convince us to buy not this but that soap, toothpaste, food, car, college, or you-name-it.

As expressed in the spirit of the original remarkably pseudo-scientific gibberish, these advertising techniques were built on "measuring subjects' reactions to messages." In the 1950s, this was done by observing eye dilations and other physiological reactions to "messages"–methods that long ago found their way into politics, with the aim of delivering more certainty in the effect of words.

So-called research data are now gathered from electrodes on potential voters who listen to political speeches, to determine the "right words" for the use of these words uniformly in talking points across a political party, which makes addressing people's real needs irrelevant–with too many in the media then repeating the juicy parts of the talking points verbatim! Anyone who doesn't think this cringeworthy and wrong on so many levels has a long way to climb back to decent human values.

The easier propagandists to call out are those who say the outright opposite of what they do. But these still seem to attract more media attention for what is said rather than done–maybe because the lie is more colorful and comes pre-packaged in a media release. Hyperbole or even mild exaggeration combined with provocative ambiguity is a headline-writer's dream, whether connected to reality or not.

More challenging is the conjurer of euphemism or maestro of the mealy-mouthed, especially those urging politicians to talk to us about "security," "peace of mind," "results," "renewal," "independence," and a litany of words being promoted into conversational currency, without the matching actions to accomplish laudable ideals. Such as "transparency" or better still "accountability" for example! Now, these sound like promising thoughts–and is it too much to ask that legislators, judiciary, and others who've sworn real oaths to do so, actually take the steps needed to **"secure** our **peace of mind** by getting a result of some accountability to deliver a renewal of democracy and individual **independence"**–at more than buggy-speed in a nano-world!? The come-ons and put-offs become encyclopedic, as the news cycle moves on.

As messages are being shaped and shared for yet another election, it's a good time to see the hucksters for who they are. Just like the about-to-be-bankrupt person in business projects confidence, even bombast, to reassure an unfortunate target to invest in a yet-again just-wonderful opportunity, so too will the political propagandist.

Waking to every day's news that includes some fearfully absurd figures, it's a time to look for what's real behind the images. Computerized propaganda has just kept improving its targeting too. And foreign state-sponsored efforts remain. So, here are some suggested rules-of-thumb to take action on, after reaching for a second cup of coffee each morning during the coming months:

1. Vote when you can.

2. Find people in your neighborhood or circle of friends and relatives, of whatever party affiliation, who believe in democracy–put aside differences, and form a coalition of ongoing-working-consultation to take actions to strengthen democracy together–and count on doing this for a long while.

3. Laugh at and/or stand up to the puffed-up and self-opinionated autocrat, whether local or (if you're able) international.

4. Write a letter (not a tweet) to your elected representatives, requesting action on something you care about, asking for and expecting a reply, and following up if you don't get one, until you do get a satisfactory (not mealy-mouthed) reply.

5. Recognize grift-language–if it really seems to be everywhere, ignore it if it looks harmless enough for now, and call it out when it's not.

6. Secure a funhouse mirror (by analogy) to hold up and show to others, yes anyone who'll listen, just how distorted and far from the common good of normalcy that the words and actions of autocrats travel.

7. Re-re-read writers like Jacques Ellul and Randal Marlin, referenced in earlier blog posts.

8. Laugh a Lot.

Tearing down grifters and their propaganda requires more than occasionally switching off the media and tech devices, although this might help gain some perspective.

Most seriously, any of us needs to take time to hold up a mirror to propaganda, to make out what's real, past the reverse/distorted images—like we do with a funhouse mirror at the sideshow, to look for the reality that's being distorted.

Not that all of this will be possible or always work—but reinforcing critical inquiry and informed challenge will prove way better than bathing every day in the distortions of people whom you'd not otherwise open your door to.

And, if enough of us believe in doing good within democracy, and communicate well, democracy will thrive.

February 15, 2022

Foreign Fake-Fun Flops

Every Dance Counts
I've **NOT** here linked or pictured the propaganda video received.
Above is a counter-image of a genuine "flash mob" dance
(one of a great many in the USA)
by Lorie Shaull, DCPantsuitPower Flash Mod Dance, Every Dance Counts
is licensed under CCA-BY-SA-2.0 Generic.
https://commons.wikimedia.org/wiki/File:DCPantsuitPower_Flash_Mob_Dance,_Every_Dance_Cou nts_(30698326112).jpg

When a foreign adversary focuses on spontaneity for a propaganda video, it's great when they don't get that they're on slippery ground.

Anyway, for the propaganda video I just received, it's even more encouraging that whoever was directing the propaganda failed to see the humungous humor in the incongruity of having a couple of hundred young folks happen to gather at a mountain-top ski-field. Then, to have them so-called spontaneously break into a "flash mob" dance, for no reason, dancing to vintage American music—with the foreign adversary's iconic buildings etc. also just happening to be in the backdrop views.

Maybe it was a further "tell" that contradicted the supposed spontaneity that on-site were a helicopter and two gigantically high bucket-cranes used to video the wide-angle shots. Oh yes, this was a big-budget production, worthy of the attention of whoever was the chief of propaganda.

There were many other "tells" in this week's video too. It was brought to the inbox by those fun-loving folks who stimulated the Berlin Wall. What's that about history repeating, and the adoration of walls? But I'm not in the business of listing out all the "tells" that would be obvious to the rest of us.

In the interests of the health of those who were the creative "talent" for the video, I hope they manage to get themselves transferred soon out of the Propaganda Bureau to the Tourism Bureau, or anywhere else-- before the failure of this propaganda flop is fully understood in the foreign propaganda bureaucracy.

The philosopher Jacques Ellul, whom I've mentioned once or twice before, warned foreign adversaries to beware of their cultural clumsiness, when it comes to launching propaganda in another country. Gotta admit this video seemed better than the foreign propaganda in Ellul's time, but that's still no compliment.

Maybe the fake in the video I just saw would slip by some folks–like the social media mob who won't pause to think, or busy folks eager for any joy amid the Covid Pandemic.

Still, the "tells" of sleaze-at-work were very many, which is good for **"we, the propagandized."**

September 27, 2020

Time to Chill

Big Brother Orwell "1984" in Donetsk, Ukraine
by Борис У is licensed under CCA-SA3.0 Unported.
https://commons.wikimedia.org/wiki/File:BigBrother.jpg

It's time... Being hooked is bad. The media are hooked, so why not us too.

Look around you—it won't take long to see someone chained to catching the latest meaningless but dangerous inanity.

Media analysts for years have noted the media's preoccupation with the big 5 = Disaster, Celebrity, Crime, Sex, and Violence.

Anytime media can capture all 5 categories in one story, especially in politics, wow, what a story! And there you have all wrapped into one what people living in New York City saw long ago. But Groundhog Day is no longer just a movie.

This is the bigger story of why it's time to ignore the nonsense. Time to tackle what matters now.

Better to take actions I've suggested in an earlier blog post. Do get out your graffiti "spray-can" of words to push back (saving energy and focus for the big lies), turn off the media for most of the day, talk to your friends, build personal networks, and... chill.

The serious observers of propaganda knew this long ago. Of course, right now the technology is already in many TVs for the 2-way scary big brother screen that Orwell warned about (not a conspiracy theory, just fact). But unlike Orwell's "Utopia=Nowhere Land," we *can* turn the screen off, for now.

Not new. As your quick google search will confirm: "Julius Caesar's influence provided Augustus with manipulative techniques he would need, such as literature, statues, monuments, and coins in order to gain preeminence in Rome."

In other words, what Ellul has warned about as the most dangerous propaganda: **social propaganda**. That is, what our preoccupations build into the social fabric, of media, conversation, education, arts, statuary, etc. of society. Sound familiar?

It's time. The future is in our hands.

July 26, 2020

Where's the Outrage?

Sydney Harbour Bridge & Opera House Fireworks
by Linh_rOm is licensed under CCA-BY-2.0 Generic.
https://commons.wikimedia.org/wiki/File:Sydney_habour_bridge_%26_opera_house_fireworks_new_year_eve_2008.jpg

Perhaps the most substantial failure in public communication during recent decades is the not-so-combined effort to counter the death-cult of anti-vax and anti-mask propagandists, in the United States and more widely.

Since the first vaccinations against Covid commenced one year ago yesterday in this country, we've been presented with countless images on television and social media that show people being jabbed with a needle.

The media latched on to this image early. The first person vaccinated on national TV here was a nurse, who had the good sense immediately afterwards to clap her hands and nonverbally try to convey joy, as best she could from behind her mask. On-screen vaccinations of some national leaders and a few celebrities progressively followed, laudably showing the right thing to do. Then a strange series of giveaways and gimmicks were popped in front of viewers as incentives—thereafter followed continuous urgings to vaccinate, alongside repeated diatribes on dire consequences of not vaccinating.

One year later when dealing with Covid, what remains as the dominant visual on all media here is the image of needles going into arms—this is NOT enticing, even possibly for masochists. Conjecturing that this contributes some *ad populum* appeal is just too feeble to treat seriously.

Worse still, this visual sets the frame for the sometimes white-coated experts urging vaccination. The only other visual with much prominence is a tufted ball ominously floating through some micro-universe, presumably to represent Covid magnified under a microscope, and on its way to infecting someone. Does anyone really think this conveys confidence in science?

As the world continues to face the worst pandemic in living memory, what is outrageous is the failure to learn from so many well-documented, successful public health campaigns—strategies and insights readily available from decades of encouraging better behaviors on smoking, drink-driving, skin-cancer prevention, swimming pool fencing, and a host of other public health concerns.

Among the many early anti-smoking campaigns that failed to work were some blanket representations of dire consequences from smoking, with dramatically graphic visuals failing to change behavior. As with any communication, creatively anticipating varieties of interpretation matter, along with testing of draft "messaging." Surely, we can do better now!

Wherever you're reading this, feel free to comment on the extent to which public communication is helping or otherwise your nation's efforts to vaccinate—which, so far, is the only way to make us all safe. Most importantly, ask your leaders and media what each will do to help.

Hoping that you keep safe over the festive season—and **let's wish for 2022 to bring better!**

December 15, 2021

From Now On

Sydney Fireworks New Year
by Rob Chandler is licensed under CCA-BY-2.0 Generic.
https://commons.wikimedia.org/wiki/File:OperaSydney-Fuegos2006-342289398.jpg

"The propagandist's first requirement is to be heard," said Jacques Ellul in 1962.

Regardless of whether or not you know much about Ellul, this observation ought to be self-evident to anyone who thinks for more than a moment about the matter.

Why then do so many media megaphones irresistibly remain servants of someone they also regularly describe as an outrageous liar? Why magnify manufactured outrage?

When facing any other serious threat, it would be a no-brainer to first remove the threat. And to be fair, some media are making headway in countering propaganda, mainly by bringing us other wanted news.

By searching out lucid opponents whom any propagandist has, perhaps more yet will elaborate better and new visions for the future, without mention of the propagandist or his outrageous fantasies.

A wonderful quality of propaganda is how quickly it decays, when denied opportunity for a "refresh."

So much "news" is still slave to the gossip formulae, named by media analysts for years, of reacting to Disaster, Celebrity, Crime, Sex, and Violence. This is sad commentary on the lack of imagination of some media and media educators when thinking of their audiences.

After too many years of countless variants of this kind of verbal and nonverbal abuse, for sure, our household will not be alone in continuing to search out the better media options.

Happy New Year!

December 27, 2020

Thinking for a Future

US propaganda poster in 1917
by James Montgomery Flagg, Library of Congress.
This image is in the Public Domain {{PD-US-expired}}
https://commons.wikimedia.org/wiki/File:FlaggWakeUpAmerica.jpg

After 1949, the world was under threat of thermonuclear annihilation following the Soviet explosion of an atomic bomb and America's commitment to develop the even more massive hydrogen bomb.

The playwright Arthur Miller, much later, wrote of this time, "An era can be said to end when its basic illusions are exhausted... The whole place was becoming inhuman, not only because an unaccustomed fear was spreading so fast, but more because nobody would admit to being afraid."

Unsurprisingly, with eyes opened and emotion keyed to the significance of our time, Americans are voting in unprecedented numbers. Time will tell how bumpy a ride the next weeks and months will be.

For the years beyond to be better, I believe some changes are needed to offset the virus of pseudo-populism, which also will NOT "just disappear." And no nation is immune. As if there's not enough to deal with in the challenges imposed through Covid and the irresponsible neglect by some wannabe leaders!

A sad lesson from the current era is that norms and the rule of law are no bulwarks against rogue actors who specialize in word-salad and obstruction that exploit the legal system for personal advantage.

With the United States now showing, more than ever before, that we can come together with family, friends, and neighbors to vote, surely to climb the next rocky mountain we need to find better paths to the future.

Central now for civil society to operate are workable ways to detect and counteract propaganda, along the lines outlined vigorously for decades. As Dorothy L. Sayers noted after the tyranny of World War II, each of us needs to be better able to disentangle "fact from opinion and the proven from the plausible."

Today, we see largely that part of the political process that politicians allow us to see. Learning what we do from politicians, illusion is imbibed by describing it to others. Worse still is when voters ignore entirely what's happening, in some mistaken belief that nothing changes whoever you vote for, as some non-voters just shared with a television reporter. With such people searching for information as a way to reduce uncertainty, so begins the cycle toward the cult.

Every society has its own illusions. It's best to truly understand how public figures shape their words and actions to relate to us. We clearly need a better basis for learning how to learn. So, some starter thoughts:

1. Education programs require strengthening of critical thinking as core to being a good citizen (and a graduate from any level of education).

2. Virtues of justice, temperance, courage, and wisdom require more effective nurture in public figures, teachers, librarians, students, parents, family, friends, neighbors, and all of us.

3. Improved civics knowledge and practical understanding of what democracy prevents are urgent needs.

Hopefully, we can agree this much at least with the warning from the remarks of Dorothy L. Sayers in 1947 that "the sole true end of education is simply this: to teach [women and] men how to learn for themselves; and whatever instruction fails to do this is effort spent in vain."

This is not about any kind of rivalry among disciplines of learning or in the teaching staffroom. By analogy, it is about the future to be found in past success—such as, over the years since 2018, the sustained efforts of students from Parkland High School in Florida—lest we forget!

October 30, 2020

Blog Post Titles, First Lines, & Dates

Page
3   The Sudden Change Continues – **In some ways akin** to the personally piercing shaft of memory each of... May 16, 2020
50   "Aotearoa" **... is often translated** from the Māori to describe New Zealand as the... May 19, 2020
52   Face Up to Absurdity – **With each passing day,** the absurd harm to lives and livelihood... May 24, 2020
117   Speaking Out – **Democracy** has a long association with communication. In... June 3, 2020
165   Imagine – **Alexander Hamilton** warned in *The Federalist, Number 8*... June 14, 2020
84   Violent Rhetoric – **Not** a new phenomenon. How about from Patrick Henry? "Give me... June 19, 2020
168   It's Time for Plain Talk – **Augustus Saint-Gaudens,** an American sculptor of the Beaux-Arts... June 25, 2020
133   Accountability – **Some time ago,** with the aim of getting attention in a lunchtime talk to a... July 1, 2020
102   We or Me? – **So, we continue...** July 12, 2020
191   Time to Chill – **It's time...** Being hooked is bad. The media are hooked, so why not us... July 26, 2020
26   What's So Funny? – **A delightful book** on *The Language of Humour* by Walter Nash just arrived... August 6, 2020
161   Silly Season – **Thanks to George Orwell's** short essay published in 1946, "Politics and... August 23, 2020
62   Change or Be Changed – **Gulliver's visit** to the Land of the Houyhnhnms, at one level is an... August 31, 2020
176   Funny That... – **Did you know** that long-time Monty Python fan and former member of... September 13, 2020
178   It's the PROPAGANDA, Stu*** – **Today's message** is to the media (and all of us, really). Here are the... September 15, 2020
189   Foreign Fake-Fun Flops – **When a foreign adversary** focuses on spontaneity for a propaganda... September 27, 2020

Page

59 Rip Van Who? – **Do you sometimes wish** you'd fallen into a long sleep early in 2020 like… September 29, 2020

47 Go High – **During this never quiet time** in the Silly Season of another election, you… October 15, 2020

197 Thinking for a Future – **After 1949,** the world was under threat of thermonuclear annihilation… October 30, 2020

67 Catnip Curse – **Germaine Greer** described herself during an Address to the National… November 12, 2020

128 Beyond Heavens – **Growing up with astronomy** as an interest was some preparation for… November 29, 2020

130 Trouble with Theory – **At the outset,** just for the record, I'm committed to theory and putting… December 2, 2020

195 From Now On – **"The propagandist's** first requirement is to be heard," said Jacques Ellul… December 27, 2020

19 Beyond Reason – **As the inexorable grind** of the United States legal processes progress in… January 13, 2021

77 What the Inaugural Address Means – **The recent inaugural address** of the new president of the United States… January 22, 2021

73 What We Say – **Way back when,** Australian schoolchildren would challenge each other… February 10, 2021

171 What to Do – **A Gary Larson cartoon** that a friend recently shared illustrates by… February 24, 2021

10 The Next Thing? – **Who knows,** with Spring trying to make it in the northern hemisphere, March 16, 2021

110 Civil Civics – **Just when the need is great,** this month more than 300 educators from… March 22, 2021

36 When Fools Rule – **Once the glory day** for pranksters, April Fool's Day seems to be less… April 1, 2021

99 Style – **The popular singer** Sting has it. Along with Aretha Franklin, Stevie… May 2, 2021

70 Why Read? Why Write? – **Answers to** "why write?" are probably as many as why we read. Whether… May 31, 2021

86 Reach – **Engaging an audience** takes talent. Whether comedian, TV anchor… June 30, 2021

109 .0001% – **Policy wonks long believed** healthcare delivery to be governed by… July 20, 2021

114 To Strengthen Democracy – **If imitation** is the sincerest form of flattery, how hugely ironic it is that… July 30, 2021

15 Five Rings – **The Olympic torch** is once more passed forward. Beyond conception as… August 9, 2021

156 Letters of Law – **A foundation** for a fair application of the law requires the interpretation… August 19, 2021

Page

31 Humor-in-Law – **Studying criminal law** way back when, a required class assignment was… September 1, 2021

96 The -ism Family – **Large, or even dangerously dominant,** in people's minds and hearts is… September 11, 2021

64 Whose Challenge? – **Often barely noticeable,** like the passing of the date on the calendar for… October 1, 2021

7 Light, or No… – **Have you ever wondered** why some people convey a sense of optimism… October 21, 2021

43 Thylacine – **No longer seen** and mostly under-appreciated was Thylacine, commonly… November 1, 2021

121 Remembrance – **United through invisible links** stronger than titanium are people who… November 15, 2021

140 Fall in the Suburbs – **At this time each year** with foliage fallen, in the early morning half-light… December 1, 2021

193 Where's the Outrage? – **Perhaps the most substantial failure** in public communication during… December 15, 2021

148 The Back-seat Driver – **Did you ever experience** in the years before Covid-19, when driving… December 29, 2021

80 Surf – **New Year for a couple of decades** marked the final stage of three-weeks… January 1, 2022

144 Pundit Propaganda – **Propagandist Pundits** play too much with our perception. Will such… January 13, 2022

12 Honestly – **Expected on full display** off the coast of Ireland this week will be a… January 30, 2022

185 The Cons – *It's all done with mirrors.* A once-famous columnist for a still-famous… February 15, 2022

41 Neighbors – **Much like family,** we don't usually get to pick our neighbors. Pleasant… February 21, 2022

39 Homage – **George Orwell** concluded his *Homage to Catalonia* with a reflection on his… March 5, 2022

54 Tales of Two – **Joan Druett** in *Tales of Two* brings to life the character of people… March 21, 2022

105 To Speak Out! – **True leaders** advance the common good, using "…truthful, lawful, and… April 7, 2022

180 Certainty Claims – **As we re-enter** the "silly seasons" of electioneering, in the United States… April 22, 2022

89 Much in Verbs – **Shakespeare's play** *Much Ado about Nothing* lightly explores human… May 9, 2022

21 Making It So – **Perhaps also honoring** this violinist's virtuoso performance from a time… May 30, 2022

150 How Anti-social Are Social Media? – **While legislators** and the providers of social media platforms quibble… June 16, 2022

Page

55 Angel to Grifter to…? – **In 1952,** the iconic educator Robert Maynard Hutchins completed… June 28, 2022

15 Vive Le Tour de France – ***Le Tour 2022*** commenced less than a week ago. Followers and fans on… July 5, 2022

92 A Few Words – **Regularly counted on** but little noticed are some words that appear to… July 15, 2022

158 Not Propaganda? – **Most attributed** to the philosopher Immanuel Kant are rules for… July 25, 2022

152 What's Real – **As far back as memory,** books and bookshelves! Being read to when… August 12, 2022

123 Speak Read Write Vote – **Regardless of such wisdom,** it was for much too long that otherwise… August 31, 2022

125 Now Is the Time – **With the many anti-democracy** propagandists still generally not held… September 16, 2022

155 Polls – **Masquerading** as breaking news this morning was the "bombshell"… October 12, 2022

28 Fabulists – **It's just as well** dictionaries pay no heed to the principle of guilt by… October 18, 2022

34 Cows & Curtains – **How delightful** that we gained another hour of light at the end of today… November 6, 2022

23 Votes for Action – **In the past week,** enough voters who identify as Independent or… November 13, 2022

1 Bestest Words? – **Words shape** ideas and feelings. Or, more truly, it's how we interpret… December 15, 2022

Bibliography

_____ (2022), *Irish Echo*, February 1
"Aunty Muriel" (2017), *Aunty Muriel's Blog*, "What is stylistics?" September 7, https://auntymuriel.com/2017/09/07/what-is-stylistics/#comments
Baines, Paul, Nicholas O'Shaughnessy, and Nancy Snow (Eds.), *The Sage Handbook of Propaganda*, Thousand Oaks, CA: Sage
BBC News (2016), "Armistice Day 2016: Sydney Opera House lit up with red poppies," November 11, https://www.bbc.co.uk/news/world-australia-37946056
Bergson, Henri (1969), 'The Comic in General: The Comic Element in Forms and Movements', in Eastman, A.M. et. al., *The Norton Reader: An Anthology of Expository Prose*, New York: W.W. Norton, pp. 716-25
Biden, Joseph R. (2021), *Inaugural Address, January 20, 2021*, Washington, DC: The White House, United States Government, www.whitehouse.gov/briefing-room/speeches-remarks/2021/01/20/inaugural-address-by-president-joseph-r-biden-jr/
Billington, Kevin (Film Director) (1970), *The Rise and Rise of Michael Rimmer*, London: David Paradine Productions, https://www.youtube.com/watch?v=fPE-vddZ-aA
Bolt, Neville (2020), "Propaganda of the Deed and Its Anarchist Origins," in Paul Baines, Nicholas O'Shaughnessy, and Nancy Snow (Eds.), *The Sage Handbook of Propaganda*, Thousand Oaks, CA: Sage, pp. 3-21
Bradbury, Malcolm (Ed.) (1998), *The Atlas of Literature*, New York: Stewart Tabori and Chang
The Bureau [original title: *Le Bureau des Légendes*] (2015), Canal+ television series https://en.wikipedia.org/wiki/The_Bureau_(TV_series)
Burnet, Ken (1993), "Relationship Fund Raising," Conference of the Fundraising Institute of Australia, Brisbane, Qld [citing Woody Allen]
Cahill, Thomas (1995), *How the Irish Saved Civilization*, New York: Nan A. Talese
Chandler, Raymond (1939), *The Big Sleep*, New York: Alfred A. Knopf
Churchill, Winston S. (1956), *The Birth of Britain*, New York: Dodd Mead
Collins, Philip (2017a), *When They Go Low, We Go High*, London: 4th Estate
Collins, Philip (2017b), 'The Art of Political Speech', Leith, Sam (interviewer), *The Spectator–podcast*, 25 October
Constructive Institute (2022), "What Is Constructive Journalism?" https://constructiveinstitute.org/what/an-additional-layer/

Constructive Journalism Project (2014), https://www.constructivejournalism.org
Crane, David (2021), "Up close and personal: voices from The Great War, week by week," *The Spectator*, February 27, https://www.spectator.co.uk/article/up-close-and-personal-voices-from-the-great-war-week-by-week/
Crystal, David, *website* – https://www.davidcrystal.com/GBR/David-Crystal
Crystal, David and Derek Davy (1969), *Investigating English Style*, London: Longman
Crystal, David (2008), *Txtng: The gr8 db8*, Oxford: Oxford University Press
Crystal, David (2016), "Orwell as Linguist," *The Orwell Lecture at Emirates Festival of Literature*, Dubai, 12 March
Cukor, George (Film Director) (1964), *My Fair Lady*, Burbank, CA: Warner Bros.
Culotta, Nino (1957), *They're a Weird Mob*, Sydney: Angus & Robertson
Druett, Joan (2019), *Island of the Lost*, Chapel Hill, NC: Algonquin
Educating for American Democracy (2021), *Educating for American Democracy Project*, https://www.educatingforamericandemocracy.org
Ellegard, Alvar (1962), *A Statistical Method for Determining Authorship*, Goteborg: Acta Universitas Gothoburgensis
Ellul, Jacques (1965), *Propaganda: The Formation of Men's Attitudes*, New York: Knopf
Fahnestock, Jeanne (2011), *Rhetorical Style: The Uses of Language in Persuasion*, New York: Oxford University Press
Flint, E. H. (1970), 'Comparison of Spoken and Written English: Towards an Integrated Method of Linguistic Description', in Ransom, W.S. (Ed.), *English Transported*, Canberra: Australian National University Press, pp. 161-87
Flower, Linda (1993), *Problem-solving Strategies for Writing*, 4th edn, Fort Worth: Harcourt Brace Jovanovich
Forsyth, Mark (2020), *What Makes a Movie Line Memorable? Diacope*, https://www.youtube.com/watch?v=oo5Ikx3F5ak
Greer, Germaine (1970), *The Female Eunuch*, London: Paladin
Greer, Germaine (1971), *Address to The National Press Club*, Washington D.C., 18 May
Hamilton, Alexander (1787), *The Federalist* No. 8, November 20
Hardy, Frank (1971), *The Outcasts of Foolgarah*, Melbourne: Allara
Hargreaves, David and Margaret-Louise O'Keefe (2021), *As We Were: The First World War: Tales from a Broken World Week-by-Week*, London: White Fox Publishing, four volumes
Hutchins, Robert Maynard (Ed.) (1952), 'A Letter to the Reader', *The Great Conversation: The Substance of a Liberal Education*, Chicago: William Benton
Hutchins, Robert Maynard (Ed.) (1952), *The Great Ideas: A Syntopicon of the Great Books of the Western World*, Volumes I & II, Chicago: William Benton
Jackson, Peter (2011), "100 words of English: How far can it get you?" 30 March, BBC News, https://www.bbc.co.uk/news/magazine-12894638
Jowett, Garth S. and Victoria O'Donnell (Eds.) (2006), *Readings in Propaganda and Persuasion: New and Classic Essays*, Thousand Oaks, CA: Sage
Jowett, Garth S. and Victoria O'Donnell (2019), 7th Edition, *Propaganda and Persuasion*, Thousand Oaks, CA: Sage

King, Martin Luther (1963), "I Have a Dream," in John Graham (Ed.), *Great American Speeches 1898-1963*, New York: Appleton-Century-Crofts, pp. 117-21 [presented August 28, 1963]

Kirby, Michael D. (2010), *The Internalisation of Domestic Law and Its Consequences, Public Conversation between The Hon Justice Antonin Scalia, Associate Justice of the Supreme Court of the United States of America and The Hon Michael Kirby, Justice of the High Court of Australia, 1996-2009*, 9 February, Website Speech No. 2441, pp. 1-21, https://www.michaelkirby.com.au/images/stories/speeches/2000s/2010_Speeches/2441.PublicConv.Scalia&Kirby9February2010.pdf

Knightley, Phillip (2003), *The First Casualty: The War Correspondent as Hero, Propagandist and Myth-Maker from the Crimea to Iraq*, London: André Deutsch

Lake, David J. (1975), *The Canon of Thomas Middleton Plays: Internal Evidence for the Major Problems of Authorship*, London: Cambridge University Press

Lewis, Michael (1999), *The New New Thing*, New York: W.W. Norton

Lewis-Kraus, Gideon (2022), "How Harmful is Social Media," *The New Yorker*, June 3, https://www.newyorker.com/culture/annals-of-inquiry/we-know-less-about-social-media-than-we-think?

Lumet, Sidney (Film Director) (1976), "I'm as mad as hell, and I'm not going to take this anymore! Speech from *Network*," Burbank, CA: Metro-Goldwyn-Mayer https://www.youtube.com/watch?v=ZwMVMbmQBug

McGee, John A. (1929), *Persuasive Speaking*, New York: Scribner's, https://archive.org/details/persuasivespeaki00mcge

Madden, Erin (2019) "The Popularization of the Yo-yo," YO-YO–The Mysteries of the Yo-Yo, Fredericksburg, Va.: University of Mary Washington, *WordPress Website*, https://historyoftech.mcclurken.org/yoyo/popularization/the-popularization-of-the-yo-yo

Marlin, Randal (2013), *Propaganda and the Ethics of Persuasion*, Peterborough, ON: Broadview

Marlin, Randal (2021), "Dynamic Tension for Pandemic Times," *Current Drift*, 10 May, IJES Elul Society, ellul.org/current-drift/dynamic-tension-for-pandemic-times/

Miller, Rodney G. (2022), "Reform Advocacy of Michael Kirby," *Australians Speak Out: Persuasive Language Styles*, Albany, NY: Parula, pp. 180-92 https://www.michaelkirby.com.au/sites/default/files/content/AustSpksOutCh15.pdf

Morton, A.Q. and M. Levison (1966), 'Some Indications of Authorship in Greek Prose', in Leed, Jacob (Ed.), *The Computer and Literary Style*, Kent, OH: Kent State University Press, pp. 141-79

Morton, A. Q. (1978), *Literary Detection: How to Prove Authorship and Fraud in Literature and Documents*, n.p.: Bowker

Nash, Walter (1985), *The Language of Humour*, New York: Longman

Orwell, George (1954), 'Principles of Newspeak', *Nineteen Eighty-Four*, Harmondsworth: Penguin, pp. 241-51 [1st published 1949]

Orwell, George (1981), 'Politics and the English Language', *A Collection of Essays*, Orlando, FL: Harvest, pp. 156-71 [1st published 1946]

Orwell, George (2018), *Homage to Catalonia*, n.p.: Bibliotech Press

Packard, Vance (1957), *The Hidden Persuaders,* New York: David McKay Company
Petelin, Roslyn (2014), *UQx Write101x English Grammar and Style*-Video, St. Lucia, Qld: University of Queensland, Website,
 https://www.youtube.com/channel/UC8qZTqvQsFomCo6xFNX7GZg
Pinker, Stephen (2019), *Proceedings National Academy of Sciences,* 116, 9, pp. 3476-81
Pomerantsev, Peter (2019), *This Is NOT Propaganda: Adventures in the War Against Reality,* London: Faber and Faber
Ricks, Thomas E. (2017), *Churchill & Orwell, The Fight for Freedom,* New York: Penguin
Sanger, David E. and Michael D. Shear (2021), "Eighty Years Later, Biden and Johnson Revise the Atlantic Charter for a New Era," *The New York Times,* June 10
Sayers, Dorothy L. (1948), *The Lost Tools of Learning: Paper Read at a Vacation Course in Education, Oxford, 1947,* London: Methuen
Schumacher, Hélène (*2020*). "Is this the most powerful word in the English language?" 31st December, BBC, https://www.bbc.com/culture/article/20200109-is-this-the-most-powerful-word-in-the-english-language
Sesame Street (2002), *Cookie's Letter of the Day E,*
 https://archive.org/details/videoplayback-2021-09-06-t-101937.912
Shakespeare, William (2016), *Much Ado about Nothing,* London: Bloomsbury [1st published 1623]
Shaw, George Bernard (2001), *Pygmalion,* New York: Washington Square Press [Her Majesty's Theatre English language premiere 1914]
Snow, Nancy and Nicholas J. Cull (Eds.) (2020), *Routledge Handbook of Public Diplomacy,* 2nd edn, New York: Routledge
Snyder, Timothy (2017), *On Tyranny: Twenty Lessons from the Twentieth Century,* New York: Tim Duggan
Sommers, Roseanna (2021), "Experimental Jurisprudence: Psychologists Probe Lay Understandings of Legal Constructs," *Science,* Vol 373:6553, 23 July, pp. 394-5
Sommers, Roseanna (2020), "Commonsense Consent," *Yale Law Journal,* Vol 129:8, pp. 2232-307
Sproule, J. Michael (1994), *Channels of Propaganda,* Bloomington, IN: EDINFO Press and ERIC Clearinghouse
Swift, Jonathan (1996), *Gulliver's Travels,* Mineola, NY: Dover [1st published 1726]
Thomas, Dylan (1944), *Quite Early One Morning,*
 https://www.youtube.com/watch?v=ayhGlv-bceY
Thomas, Dylan (1949), Reads "Poem in October" and "In My Craft or Sullen Art," Columbia LP, issued in 1950 on Columbia Masterworks label, catalogue number ML4259, https://www.youtube.com/watch?v=3XMaJanGuWI
Thurber, James (2017), *The Wonderful O,* New York: Penguin
Tobia, Kevin P. (2020), "Testing Ordinary Meaning," *Harvard Law Review,* Vol 134:726, pp. 727-806
Toffler, Alvin and Adelaide Farrell (1970), *Future Shock,* New York: Random House
Tolstoy, Leo (2019), *War and Peace,* New York: Penguin [1st published in Russian 1869, translated into English in 1886 and 1899]
Zada, John (2021), *Veils of Distortion, How the News Media Warps our Minds,* Toronto: Terra Incognita

Acknowledgments

I am especially grateful to readers of the blog, including family and friends near and far, who send comments or cartoons or notes, more than a few of which stimulate thoughts for writing. During the events of recent years, the humor and insights of many people are a tremendous support. For the efforts of all who continuously build the online resources used for this writing, my heartfelt thanks. Finally, I acknowledge the thoughtfulness, patience, and support of my wife through so many years.

About the Author

Rodney G. Miller's recent book *Australians Speak Out* is named Reviewer's Choice by Midwest Book Review senior reviewer, Diane Donovan. His other books exploring insights and priorities to strengthen communication include *Communication Essays* and *Communication & Beyond*. He is published by the State University of New York Press and The Royal Society of Queensland, with early writing in *The Australian* newspaper.

While teaching communication at Queensland University of Technology, he founded and for over a decade edited *Australian Journal of Communication*. He has since led the advancement of innovative education for universities in the United States and internationally.

By the author

Communication Essays
Communication & Beyond
Australians Speak Out: Persuasive Language Styles
Finding a Future

Website: communicator.rodney-miller.com

INDEX

A

absurd(ity), 45, 52-3, 106, 145, 187
accolade, 185
accountable, 60, 63, 125, 137
    accountability, 2, 19, 23, 56, 124, 130-2, 133-5, 183, 186-7
ad populum, 173, 194
adjective(s), 74, 91
address, inaugural *see* inaugural address,
adverb(s), 74, 78, 90, 91, 181
Aesop, 28, 68, 141
Aladdin, 91
All Blacks, 95
Allen, Woody, 176
ally, 33
America, 24, 44, 88, 90, 133, 135, 197
    American(s), 4, 24, 33, 59, 168, 189, 198
    democracy, American, 119
    North, 15, 82
    president, 78
    South, 15
amoral, 67-8, 159
analogy, 46, 67-8, 81, 166, 171, 188, 199
anaphora, 78, 105
anarchism, 45, 96
Andersen, Hans Christian, 28
anecdote, 26
angel, 56-7
Anglo-centric, 27
animal(s), 44, 140
Animal Farm, 28, 168
animal control, 68
Antarctic, 15, 99
"anti-," 23, 181-3
anti-democracy, 60, 125, 181
antidote, 1
anti-hero, 106
anti-mask, 65, 98, 193
anti-smoking, 194
anti-social, 150
anti-vax, 65, 98, 193
antitheses, 78
Aoraki/Mt. Cook, 95
Aotearoa, 50

April Fools' Day, 36-7
Aquinas, 58
AR-15, 84-5, 103
article, 92
arts, 100, 168, 192
As We Were, 122
Asian, 43, 57, 88, 159
Astaire, Fred, 99
astronomer(s), 128-9, 152
Athens, 85
Atkinson, Sallyanne, 108
Atlantic Charter, 22
Auckland Islands, 54-5
audience, 2, 31, 66, 86-8, 101
    attention of, 94, 105
    media, 142-3, 159, 196
    propagandized, 163-4, 166
    targeting of, 179, 182
    -testing of, 79, 145
Aunty Muriel's Blog, 101
Aussie, 73, 81
Australia(ns), 34, 43-4, 53, 80-2, 88, 90, 94
    Speak Out, 105-8
    election(s), 180
    English, 75
    freedom of information, 135
authoritarianism, 97
Austen, Jane, 10
Austin A30, 31
author(s), 20, 54, 70, 82, 110
autocrat(s), 8, 48-9, 61, 125-6, 138, 150, 159-60, 187-8
axe, 67
Axis Powers, 39

B

bad, 48, 57, 191
    actor, 53, 60, 75, 85, 132, 170, 177
    behavior, 19
    words, 145
Baldwin, James, 82
ballot(s), 29-30, 126
banality, 27
barbarian, 29, 85, 89
Bassey, Shirley, 99

BBC, 53, 93, 168
beach, 11, 80-1, 91
The Beatles, 176
Beecher, Henry Ward, 86-8
beer, 43, 46
Beethoven, 99
behaviorism, 98
Bennis, Warren, 162
Benny, Jack, 99
Bergman, Ingrid, 99
Bergson, Henri, 27
Berlin Wall, 190
Biden, Joseph R, 75, 77
"the big lie," 175, 192
billabong, 81
biodiversity, 22
bird brain, 36-7
Blake, William, 43
Blue Peter, 143
bluebird, 21
"bone-shakers," 152
boogie board(s), 80
book(s), 2, 29-30, 44, 70-2, 80, 109-12, 152-3, 171-2
  commentary on:
    Australians Speak Out, 105-8
    The Female Eunuch, 67-8
    Great Books of the Western World, 56
    The Hidden Persuaders, 141
    Homage to Catalonia, 7-9, 39
    How the Irish Saved Civilization, 13
    Island of the Lost, 54-5
    The Language of Humour, 26-7
    The Lost Tools of Learning, 1, 45, 49, 198, 199
    The New New Thing, 10
    Persuasive Speaking, 66
    Propaganda, 114, 160, 141, 175, 182, 192
    Propaganda and the Ethics of Persuasion, 116, 160, 163, 164
    Propaganda & Persuasion, 160
    The Sage Handbook of Propaganda, 23
    This Is NOT Propaganda, 158-9
    Txting: The gr8 db8, 75
    Veils of Distortion, 141-3
    When They Go Low, We Go High, 47
    The Wonderful O, 28-30
Bose, Subhas Chandra, 91
bottle, 64, 67
Bow, Clara, 99
boxing, 68
Bradbury, Ray, 70
brain, 138, 141, 146, 151, 175, 177
breaking news *see* news
Brisbane, 108, 152
Britain *see* United Kingdom
B-roll, 2, 170
Brown, Charlie, 99
Bugs Bunny, 99
The Bureau, 159
Burns, Robert, 82
bystander, 61

C

Caesar, Julius, 192
Campbells and McDonalds, 97
Camus, Albert, 47
cannibalism, 97
Capitol, 19, 33
caravan, 80
care, 15, 30, 41, 48, 49, 63, 65, 97, 104, 111, 131, 135, 153, 187
  health, 48, 60, 65, 102, 109, 149, 159
  careful, 54, 59, 88, 90, 98, 120
cartoonist, 42, 172
Castro, 48
cat, 29, 67-8
catnip, 67-8
Catskill Mountains, 59
celebrity, 57, 191, 196
champion, 97
Chandler, Raymond, 61
Chaplin, Charlie, 99, 161
charlatan(s), 57, 65, 133, 142, 143, 145
choice, 58, 100, 104, 129, 166-7, 181
  of language, 74-5, 86-7, 100, 106
Churchill, Sir Winston, 7-9, 14, 22, 48, 87, 91, 123, 169
"churnalism," 142

citizen(s), 51, 52, 57, 118, 119-20, 133, 135, 172, 199
civics, 72, 118, 119-20, 131, 199
climate, 22, 93
    political, 131, 166
clock(s), 34
coat of arms, 43, 46
Cockneys, 81
Collins, Philip, 47-9
communication, 6, 29, 71, 75, 92, 100, 117, 133, 159, 162
    failure, 193
    and democracy, 117
    and propaganda, 60, 163, 181
    personalized, 170
    public, 1, 5, 37, 44-6, 62, 90, 115, 161, 194
    style, 77-9, 128-9
communism, 96
the cons, 185
Congress
    hearings, 134
    representative, 181
conjunction, 78
connotations, 153
conquest, 39-40, 89
conservatism, 96
constitution, 57, 93, 133
convention, 57, 68
Cook, Peter, 156
Cookie Monster, 30
corporatism, 97
counterstatement, 26
coup, 172
courage, 15, 17, 54, 57, 60, 118, 122, 183, 199
court, 19, 31, 94, 110, 138
    supreme, 93, 130
covid-19, 4, 21, 50, 52, 63, 85, 90, 102, 148, 167
craven, 65
creativity, 46, 72, 97
crime, 57, 191, 196
criminal(s), 20, 31-3, 137
"cringeworthy," 100, 169, 186

cronyism, 97
crook(s), 57, 85, 134, 177
crowd, 11, 84-5, 103-4, 124
Crystal, David, 75, 101, 161, 174
Culotta, Nino, 81
cult, 173, 193, 198
cultism, 97
Curtin, John, 88
custom, 57
cyclist(s), 17-8, 75, 170
cynic, 65
Czech, 29

D

daffodil, 10
Daffy Duck, 99
Danish, 29
Darwin, Charles, 71, 82
daylight saving time, 34
death, 5, 57, 84, 91
death-cult, 193
delay, 75, 170, 177, 184
delusion, 153, 172, 178, 184
democracy, 1-2, 23, 47, 57, 61, 106, 114, 117-8, 119-20, 130
    anti-, 125, 181, 187-8
    denial, 30
    guardrails of, 143
    liberté, égalité, and *fraternité,* 18
    and propaganda, 164
    roots of, 123-4
    representative, 85, 105, 130, 134-5, 138
    undermining of, 72, 145, 159-60, 172
    white-ants of, 56, 172
denial(s), 30, 184
denialism, 97
depression, 8, 19
despot(s), 61,
diacope, 82
"dial sessions," 103
dialectic, 45, 57
dictator, 161, 165, 169
dignity, 8, 58, 93, 122
dinosaur, 70, 111

disaster(s), 5, 44, 57, 191, 196
discourse, 35, 101
disinformation, 22, 142-3,
distortion(s), 65, 141-2, 182, 184, 188
"dog, black," 8
dogma, 174, 184
dog-walkers, 59
Donald Duck, 42
doubletalk, 169
doublethink, 169
Druett, Joan, 54-5
dustbin, 98, 169
Dutch, 29
Dylan, Bob, 99

E

education, 5, 45, 49, 57, 63, 64, 116, 118, 129, 199
   civics, 72, 119-20
   propaganda, 160-1, 192
educator(s), 2, 45, 49, 56, 116, 119, 196
Educating for American Democracy, 119-20
EEZ-exclusive economic zone, 12-4
elected representative, *see* politician
elitism, 98
Elizabeth I, HRH, 90
Elizabeth II, HRH *see* Queen Elizabeth
Elull, Jacques, 44, 60, 114-5, 141, 147, 160, 161-4, 166-7, 171, 173-5, 182, 188, 190, 192, 195
Elysian Fields, 75
emerald isle, 14
emotion(s), 27, 62, 97, 107, 172, 174, 184, 198
empathy, 27
English, 29, 45, 75, 78, 92, 115, 129, 146, 161
ennui, 11
environmentalism, 96
era, 37, 133, 198
Esslin, Martin, 53, 145
Europe(an), 17, 57, 74, 82, 89, 126
evangelism, 97, 196
"extaticism," 98

F

Fable(s), 28, 59, 68, 141
fabulist, 28
fact(s), 32-3, 45, 60, 66, 87, 100, 136, 156, 164, 175, 179, 192, 198
   fact-checking, 37, 65, 75, 169-70, 183
   post-fact, 159
Fahnestock, Jeanne, 101
fairness, 15
family, 31, 35, 41, 61, 71, 80, 93, 101, 158, 199
   -ism, 96-8
fantasy, 29, 111, 141, 146, 169
farmer, 34, 178
fascism, 39, 96
felonies, 103
The Female Eunuch, 67-8, 107
fence(s), 42
Fifth Column, 40
fight, 20, 67, 84, 91, 106, 134, 143, 172, 182
figurative language, 81, 178
Filene, Edward A., 160
First Nations, 106-7
fishermen, 12-4
Fleay, David, 44
Fletcher, 20
Flint, E.H., 75
Florida, 102, 161, 199
Flower, Linda, 72
flu, *see* influenza
fly, 27
de La Fontaine, Jean, 28
FOI *see* freedom of information
fool, 36, 82, 90, 169
foolishness, 37, 174
food, 48, 55, 60, 112, 179, 186
Forsyth, Mark, 82-3
founder(s), 93, 134
fragment, sentence, 75, 78
France, 5, 17-8, 90, 135, 180
Frankfurter, Justice, 137
Franklin, Aretha, 99

freedom(s), 1, 8, 30, 48, 60, 87, 91, 114, 115, 121-2, 143, 146, 179, 183
freedom of information, 135
French, 27, 29, 45, 90, 161, 166
friend(s), 4-6, 15, 35, 41, 61, 80, 81, 88, 93, 110, 122, 158, 170, 187, 192, 199
"friendliness," 32
Frow, Professor John, 174
fundamentalism, 97
funny, 6, 26, 36, 176
funny-bone, 26

G

Gandhi, Mahatma, 88
games *see* olympics
German, 29, 53, 90, 145
gerrymanders, 35
Gilbert, Kevin, 107
Gilbert and Sullivan, 32, 141
Gillard, Julia, 108
glasses, 76, 103
Goebbels, 161, 164, 170
goldfish, 65
Gordon, Harry, 110
Gorman, Amanda, 100
gossip, 19, 62, 182, 196
government, 51, 55, 57, 114, 131, 135, 149
    Australian, 94
    democratic, 33, 115, 117
    foreign, 65, 150
    United States, 181
    Westminster, 134
grace, 15
grammar, 45, 71-2, 75, 174
Great Books of the Western World, 56
Great Depression, 39,
Greer, Germaine, 67, 88, 91, 107
grief, 93, 100
grifter(s), 56, 57, 65, 124, 142, 143, 145, 188
grotesques, 106
Brothers Grimm, 28
Groundhog Day, 181, 191
Gulliver, 62, 86
gutter(s), 80, 141

H

habit, 66, 71, 95, 146
hackathon, 111-2
"hail mary," 68
halloween, 30
Hamilton, Alexander, 123, 165
Hancock, Herbie, 99
handwringing, 85, 134, 135
happiness, 22, 57, 85, 103, 158
Harrison, George, 176
Hardy, Frank, 82
Hatch Act, 63
Hatfields and McCoys, 97
health, 1, 5, 26, 48, 60, 65, 115, 179, 190, 194
    healthcare, 109, 65, 149, 159
hedonism, 98
hell, 20, 166
Hellespont, 85, 89
hellward, 144
Henry, Patrick, 84, 91
Hepburn, Audrey, 73, 99
Her Majesty's pleasure, 32
Heston, Charlton, 99
Higgins, Professor Henry, 74
High Court of Australia, 93, 108
history, 14, 18, 54-5, 85, 89-90, 98, 119-20, 152, 160, 190
Hitler, 40, 48, 53, 88, 145
Hobbes, Thomas, 44
Hollywood, 99
Homage to Catalonia, 7-9, 39
honesty, 13, 60, 103
hope, 1, 8, 13, 24, 29, 36, 55, 79, 81, 94, 102, 158, 159, 162, 199
Horsemen of the Apocalypse, 129
houyhnhnms, 62
Howard, John, 108
Hudson, Henry, 59
hula-hoop, 173
humor, 1, 26-7, 29, 31, 33, 35, 36, 48, 81, 89, 105, 106, 176, 181, 189
Humpty Dumpty, 136
Hungarian, 29
Hutchins, Robert Maynard, 56-7

215

I

ideal(s), 23, 98, 153, 185, 186
ideology, 45, 97, 101, 161, 170, 184
illusion, 129, 199
imagination, 17, 27, 30, 49, 81, 165-7, 196
imperative, 70, 78, 91, 146
inaugural address, 75, 77
incongruity, 27, 189
independence, 82, 106, 186, 187
individualism, 97, 175
infinitive, 78, 91
influenza, Spanish, 4-5
injury, 27, 36
The Inky Fool, 82
insult, 13, 27, 146, 183
interpolation, 78
Irish, 12-4, 103
Irish Echo, 14
Island of the Lost, 54-5
-ism, 96
Isocrates, 47, 72
"It-girl," 99

J

Jackson, Glenda, 100
jargon, 106
jazz, 99
jellyfish, 73
job, 48, 60, 100
joggers, 59
joke, 6, 26
journalism, 2, 87
    constructive, 2, 154, 159
journalist(s), 2, 24, 37, 44, 45, 86, 109, 142, 149, 154, 159, 181
Jowett, Garth S, 160
"joyism," 98
judge(s), 97, 136
juggernaut, 1, 62
justice, 1, 2, 57, 60, 77, 118, 138, 183, 199

K

Kamensky, Professor Jane, 120
kangaroo, 43, 105
karate, 67-8
Keating, Paul, 95, 107
Kelly, Grace, 99
Kennedy, 7
    John F., 48, 87, 91
king, 93
    almost-, 29
King Jr, Martin Luther, 48, 87, 90, 117
Kirby, Justice Michael, 94, 95, 108
Knightley, Phillip, 13

L

Lao-Tzu, 162
laggard, 66
Lalor, Peter, 84
language(s), 82, 90-1, 92, 97-8, 100-1, 136-7, 161
    analytical, 77-8
    anti-democratic, 181
    Australian, 81
    choice(s), 75, 87, 100-1, 102-4
    connotation, 74
    conventional, 72
    figurative, 81, 178-9
    inappropriate, 159, 187
    intuitive, 77-8
    lessons, 72
    and life, 100
    persuasive, 94, 105-8, 164
    political, 60, 98, 114, 115, 118, 161, 146, 158, 185-6
    and pundits, 145-7
    sexist, 57
    spoken, 75
    style, 82, 100-1, 105-8
    and thought, 70, 98, 115, 164
Larson, Gary, 171
Latin, 29, 45
Latvian, 29
laugh, 27, 70, 153, 187, 181, 188
law, 1, 2, 19-20, 31-2, 35, 57, 77, 85, 116, 124, 131, 134, 136-8, 183, 198
lawful speech, 72, 105-8, 183
lawyer(s), 32, 61
Laxness, Halldór, 82
le tour de France, 17-8

leader(s), 10, 39, 48, 50-1, 52-3, 54-5, 61, 65, 68, 78, 103, 105, 116, 129, 162-3, 166, 169, 172, 193-4, 198
learning, 45, 49, 67, 71, 198-9
Leich, Sam, 47
Letterman, David, 99
lever, tire, 67
liar(s), 28, 60, 170, 195
liberalism, 96
libertarianism, 96
liberté, égalité, and *fraternité,* 18
liberty, 22, 57, 84, 85, 91, 103, 123, 125, 165, 168
librarian(s), 26, 152, 199
library, 26-7, 110-2, 152
lies, 29, 39, 88, 90, 118, 144, 145, 170, 175, 179, 182, 184
    "the big lie, 175, 192
life, 1, 5, 21-2, 33, 44, 54, 71, 85, 89, 100, 103, 116, 145
    better, 8, 11, 39, 50, 91, 162
    civilized, 47
    daily, 57, 115
    positives, 179
    real, 141, 159
Life of Brian, 176
Liggett, Phil, 17
"likes," 173
Lincoln, 48, 117
Linguist(s), 74, 75, 101, 161
liquor, 59
literature, 28, 89, 100, 110, 161, 192
    reviews, 151
logic, 45, 57, 78, 116
Looney Tunes, 43
Lord of the Flies, 55
love, 57, 122, 123, 128, 158
    of words, 71
luck, 33, 64, 83
Lyons, Dame Enid, 88

M

MacLean, Eleanor, 164
madness, 42
Mandala, 48
maneuvers, 13, 35

Mao, 48
māori, 50
marlboro man, 46
Marlin, Randal, 115, 116, 160, 163-4, 188
Marlowe, 20
Marquess of Queensberry rules, 67
martian, 104
Marx, Groucho, 99
masochism, 98
McCarthyist-like, 72
McGee, John A, 86
me, 102-415
media, 115, 124, 134, 141-3, 145, 149, 153-4, 156, 166, 170, 177, 178, 183-4, 186, 191-2, 193-4, 195-6
    social, 62, 102, 109-11, 115, 150-1, 169, 172, 175, 184, 190
media freak, 67
meme(s), 6, 134
Memorial Day, 22, 122
Menzies, Sir Robert, 88, 94, 107
message, 100, 111, 142, 159, 162, 166, 169, 186-7
metaphor, 8, 82, 97, 105
Middleton, 20
Miller, Arthur, 198
Miller, Clyde R., 160
mirror(s), 185, 188
misinformation, 45
mob, 18, 19-20, 81, 115, 181, 189-90
modernism, 97
monarchy, 18, 138, 164
monolog, 45-6
Montagues and Capulets, 97
Montesquieu, 117
Monty Python, 176
Morrison, Scott, 108
Moses, 110
Mozart, 99
Much Ado about Nothing, 89
Murphy, Pat, 12-4
My Fair Lady, 73-4
myth, 13, 48, 128-9, 134, 141, 181
mythology, 128-9

N

Napoleon, 41
Nash, Ogden, 141
Nash, Walter, 26-7
nasties, 29
National Academy of Sciences, 78, 129
National Library of New Zealand, 110
National Press Club, Washington DC, 67, 95, 107
National Reading Association, 72
nationalism, 97
Nazism, 97
Nehru, Jawaharlal, 88
neighbor(s), 35, 41-2, 57, 61, 102-3, 140-1, 158, 172, 187, 199
neologism, 97
Netherlands, 90, 126, 135
New Guinea, 43
New Year, 80, 83, 193, 195-6
New Yorker, 150-1
The New York Times, 22
New Zealand, 5, 50, 54, 92, 95, 110-1, 135
news, 2, 46, 71, 90, 110, 141-3, 153-4, 155, 169, 179, 187, 195-6
   breaking, 2, 10, 62, 155, 177
   constructive, 2, 154, 159
   newspaper(s), 4, 44, 90, 110, 118, 144, 152-3, 185
9/11, 4, 98, 172
Nixon, Richard, 88
nonsense, 61, 65, 115, 182, 191
Norway, 98
Norwegian, 29
"not us," 182
noun(s), 74, 90, 91, 146
novel(s), 81, 152
nudism, 98

O

O, 28-30
O'Donnell, Victoria, 160
offspring, 150, 161, 170
O'Grady, John, 81
oligarchy, 57
Oodgeroo Noonuccal, 88, 91, 107
olympic(s), 15-6, 106
opponent(s), 8, 61, 68, 94, 112, 164, 169, 195
   character assassination of, 182
ornithorhynchus, 73
originalism, 93, 97, 137
Orwell, George, 7-9, 28, 39, 44, 60, 98, 114-5, 118, 146, 158, 161, 168-9, 174, 192
The Outcasts of Foolgarah, 82
outrage, 2, 37, 45, 72, 78-9, 115, 129, 144, 153, 172, 179, 184, 193-4, 195
overstatement, 26
Oxford, 29, 45, 49
Oxonian, 29

P

Pacific, 106, 107
Packard, Vance, 60, 141
pandemic, 1, 4, 16, 52, 65, 66, 106-8, 148, 190, 194
Pankhurst, 48, 90
parallelism, 78
paralympian(s), 16
parent(s), 71, 150, 199
Parkland High School, 161, 199
parody, 26, 35
participles, 78
patient(s), 61, 102, 149, 159
peace, 103, 167, 186-7
Pericles, 48,
personality, 74, 87, 101, 183
Petelin, Roslyn, 71, 72, 174
phrase(s), 78, 81, 93
platypus, 44, 73, 105
play, 27, 34, 59, 71, 124, 129, 144, 174
play(s), theatrical, 20, 74, 89, 198
playbook, 126, 172
Play School, 143
podcast, 2, 46, 47, 48
poetry, 152
Pogo, 149
polemic, 35, 105
police, 4, 5, 20, 31-2, 33

politician(s), 11, 27, 34-5, 37, 94, 103, 118, 131, 137, 142, 154, 159, 162, 174, 177, 186, 198
 elected representative(s), 40, 46, 61, 65, 103, 133-5, 142-3, 181, 187
poll(s), 10, 35, 125, 155-6
Pomerantsev, Peter, 154, 158-60
populism, 45, 97, 115, 138, 198
 populist, 47, 72, 114, 129
 pseudo-populism, 23, 94
Port Arthur, 108
postal services, 60, 123, 163
postmodernism, 97
preposition, 78
president, 24, 37, 75, 77-8, 93, 145
 speechwriter to, 185
press, 37, 67, 95, 107
 foreign, 88
 tabloid, 100, 154
prime minister, 51, 93, 94, 106-8
 speechwriter to, 48
princesses, 106
principle(s), 26-7, 28, 48-9, 57, 115, 118, 135, 174
 democratic, 138
 persuasive, 66
 writing, 70, 72
professionalism, 97
progress, 19, 32-3, 51, 94, 124
pronoun, 78, 104
propaganda, 1-2, 24, 53, 60, 65, 89-90, 112, 133, 158-60, 161, 163-4, 165-6
 amplification of, 142
 and fashion, 173
 counter-, 115-6, 123-4, 131, 143, 144-7, 169-70, 176-7, 180-4, 185-8, 198
 of deed, 23
 foreign, 189-90
 limits of, 114
 social, 141, 192
Propaganda, 160, 174
Propaganda and the Ethics of Persuasion, 116, 160, 163
Propaganda & Persuasion, 160

propagandist(s), 49, 61, 66, 72, 85, 125, 158-60 172-5, 178-9, 193, 195
prosecution(s), 131, 143
 director of public prosecutions, 20
public, 118, 131, 135, 169
 accountability,
 corruption, 131
 diplomacy, 160
 figure(s), 2, 27, 94, 131, 138, 145, 161, 162, 199
 good, 45
 health, 194
 information, 166
 library, 152
 relations, 46, 133
 responsibility, 133
 scrutiny, 85, 118, 130
 servants, 85, 131
 talk, 1, 85, 94, 118, 162, 164, 168
pun, 26-7,
pundit(s), 29, 44-5, 85, 144-7, 150, 155, 162, 174, 183
punishment, 57, 85, 134
Pygmalion, 74

Q

Queen Elizabeth [II], 100
quibble(s), 51, 150, 163

R

radio, 36, 46, 53, 78, 107, 145
racism, 97
radicalism, 96
realism, 97
 laggards, 66
 realities, 8-9, 89, 111, 152-4, 161
 reality, 45-6, 60, 63, 65, 79, 124, 138, 141, 149, 158-60, 169, 182-4, 179, 185-8
reason, 19, 27, 57, 62, 107, 126, 152, 164, 189
relativism, 44, 97
The Remarkables, 50, 92, 95
restaurant, 27
rhetoric, 28, 57
 deceptive, 162

devices, 78, 105
  as endowment, 47
  study/teaching of, 45, 49, 82, 86-7, 101, 152
  violent, 84
rhyming substitution(s), 81
rhythm(s), 8, 26, 82
Reagan, 48
Riefenstahl, Leni, 161, 170
Ricks, Thomas E., 8-9
riot, 19-20
The Rise and Rise of Michael Rimmer, 156
road, 17-8, 32, 85, 103, 140, 153, 170
roadmap, 119-20
Rodgers and Hammerstein, 74
Rogers, Ginger, 99
Roosevelt, Eleanor, 108
Roosevelt, Franklin D., 22, 91
rose, red, 18
The Royal Society, 166
Rudd, Kevin, 107
rumor(s), 44, 46, 115, 173, 175
Rumpole of the Bailey, 31
Russians, 14

S

sadism, 98
safety, 98, 123, 131, 149, 153, 179, 183
The Sage Handbook of Propaganda, 23
Saint-Gaudens, Augustus, 168
Sayers, Dorothy, 1, 45, 198, 199
Scalia, Associate Justice, 94
school, 35, 63, 71, 121, 152, 159, 161, 173, 174, 183, 199
schoolchildren, 73, 108
schooling, 45, 72, 81
schoolkid(s), 73, 75, 173
science, 76, 129, 131, 136, 169, 194
scrutiny, 19, 85, 118, 130, 158, 183
Seattle, 4, 5
seesaw, 46
Seneca, 91
sense, 15, 18, 28, 32, 57, 94, 125, 140, 145, 193
  of belonging, 41
  of care, 153
  commonsense, 10, 97, 137, 138
  of humor, 106
  of independence, 106
  of optimism, 7
  of reality, 169
sentence(s), 73, 74-5, 78, 81, 87, 100, 106
Sesame Street, 30, 143
sex, 57, 191, 196
sexism, 27, 97, 106, 108
  sexist language, 57
Shakespeare, 20, 89, 93, 110
sharks, 73
Shaw, George Bernard, 74
shelter, 54-5, 60, 179
Sherwen, Paul, 17
shoelace, 31-2
silly season, 47, 156, 161-2, 180
skepticism, 183
sleepwalking, 60
slurs, 46
snakes, 73
Snow, Nancy, 160
"snowbird," 102
South Pacific, 106
Spanish, 12
  Civil War, 8, 39
  influenza, 4-5
Spark, Muriel, 10
speech(es), 47-8, 53, 78, 145, 87-8, 90, 95, 100, 105-8, 117, 124
  freedom of, 22, 122, 143, 145, 183
  political, 185-6
  truthful, lawful, and just, 72, 183
speechwriter, 48, 87, 100, 185
spiders, 73
sport(s), 15, 68, 152, 173
spring, 10-1, 21, 34, 93
Sproule, J. Michael, 160
St. Helena, 41
Stalingrad, 164
Stanford University, 52
Statue of Liberty, 125
Steinem, Gloria, 91
Sting, 99

student(s), 26, 71-2, 87, 111-2, 120, 137, 161, 199, 199
style, 75, 77-8, 82, 87, 99-101, 105-8, 129
stylometry, 20
summer, 11, 15, 80, 88
superheroes, 106
The Supreme Court [USA], 93, 130
surf, 80-3
surprise, 20, 71, 82, 107, 110
swan, black, 10
Sweden, 20, 90, 135
Swedish, 29
Swift, Johnathan, 62, 74
Sydney Harbour Bridge, 193, 195
Sydney Opera House, 122
symphony, 21-2
Szymborska, Wisława, 82

T

tactic(s), 17, 182
tale(s), 28-9, 54-5, 91
talent, 86-7, 99, 111, 142, 151, 167, 190
talk, 94, 98, 111, 133-4, 143, 144, 147, 149, 153, 174, 192
   distorted, 124
   doubletalk, 169
   plain, 105, 168-9
   public, 1, 85, 94, 118, 162, 164, 168
   talking points, 103, 162, 186
   trash-, 114-5
Tasmanian Devil, 43
Tasmanian Tiger, 43-6
teachers, 86, 97, 199
television, 31, 78, 93, 115, 133-4, 141, 155, 159, 170, 173, 192, 193, 198
"tell," 48-9, 60, 100-1, 115, 189, 190
temperance, 57, 60, 118, 183, 199
tense, 74, 91
terrorist(s), 20, 33, 171-4, 182
Thayer, Lee, 162
theory, 27, 63, 128, 130, 192
theater of the absurd, 52-3, 145
They're a Weird Mob, 81
thinking, 87, 90, 98, 100, 174, 196-9
   critical, 112, 115-6, 199

mono-, 160
Thomas, Dylan, 82
thought, 70, 71, 82, 87, 91 118, 146
   freedom of, 22, 115, 122, 143, 146, 183
   independent, 1, 175
   and propaganda, 163, 169, 182, 183, 195, 198
threat, 1, 13, 23-4, 44, 65, 85, 98, 124, 159, 172, 182
3D-glasses, 103
Thunberg, Greta, 100
Thurber, James, 28-30, 141
Thylacine, 43-4
Toffler, Alvin, 64
Toffler, Heidi, 64
Tolstoy, Leo, 10, 51
tone, 75, 78, 87, 89, 101
tragedy, 17, 98
tram, dropcentre, 152
tribalism, 97, 169
triffids, 179
Trollope, Anthony, 10
truth, 1-2, 13, 28, 37, 57, 72, 77, 105-6, 114, 118, 121, 145, 170, 179, 183
TV *see* television
tweet(s), 135, 168, 170, 178, 187
tyranny, 57, 121, 198
tyrant(s), 29, 57, 85, 90, 121, 123, 164

U

uber, 110
understatement, 26
United States, 1, 5, 19, 22, 34, 44, 45, 56, 65, 72, 106-7, 135, 155, 163, 193
   accountability in, 130-1, 137
   civics education, 119-20
   constitution, 93, 133
   elections, 112, 123, 125, 143, 161-2, 180-1
   president, 77, 93, 145
   resilience, 23-4
   terrorists, 33, 115, 171, 174
Universal Declaration of Human Rights, 48
utopia, 20, 47, 48-9, 192

V

vaccination, 10, 183, 193-4
vacuum, 45
Vader, Darth, 125-6
value(s), 12-3, 27, 41, 51, 56-7, 62, 77, 129, 163, 172, 182-3, 186
    democratic, 121, 181, 184
    language, 98
    social media, 150-1
    reading and writing, 72, 174
verb, 74, 78, 89-91, 146, 181
Villanova University, 26
My Cousin Vinny, 32
violence, 19, 23-4, 57, 85, 150-1, 191, 196
violin, 21
virtue(s), 48, 118, 199
virtuoso, 21
virus, 51, 149, 166, 178, 198
volkswagen, 95
volunteer, 39, 135
vote, 156, 180, 182, 184, 186, 187, 198
vax, 8, 65, 98, 193

W

wannabe, 29, 61, 65, 114-6, 123, 172, 181, 184, 198
waiter, 27
war, 2, 8, 13, 39, 57, 59, 122, 159, 165
War and Peace, 51
war-gamers, 12
Washington DC, 67, 87, 95, 107, 117, 130
wave(s), 80-3
Wayne, John, 99
we, 102-4
"we the people," 24, 27, 37, 48, 104, 124, 172-3, 181
Westminster, 134
whack-a-mole, 183
whistleblower(s), 24, 85, 131
Whitlam, Gough, 88, 95, 107
Wikipedia, 44, 169
wild west, 46
Winkle, Rip Van, 59
wisdom, 47, 53, 58, 60, 89, 93, 118, 123, 131, 155, 162, 174, 183, 199
Wizard of Oz, 184
wombat, 27
wonks, 109-11
World War I, 121-2
World War II, 22, 53, 107, 198
word(s), 1-2, 13, 17, 28-9, 80-3, 92-5, 130, 198
    accountability for, 19-20, 72
    choice of, 7-9, 74-5, 86-7, 100, 103, 106, 71, 105-6, 185-6
    connotation of, 73-6, 96-8, 153-4
    content and function, 77-9, 91, 181
    interpretation of, 136-7
    and propaganda, 145-6, 169-70, 172, 184, 192
    and reality, 160, 161
    visual, 18
    word-salad, 1-2, 9, 198
world, 81, 82, 86, 90-1, 98, 100, 106-8, 121, 129, 141, 151, 158-9, 162, 166, 172, 173, 176, 187, 194, 197
World Expo '88, 108
Wonder, Stevie, 99
Wright, Judith, 82
writer(s), 50, 70-1, 74-5, 82, 86-7, 91, 105
    fable, 28
    headline, 90, 186
    on propaganda, 23, 160, 166, 174, 188
    speechwriter, 48, 87, 100, 185

X

Xerxes, 85, 89-90
x-ray glasses, 76

Y

yahoos, 62-3
yo-yo, 173

Z

Zada, John, 141-2
Zen, 10
zombies, 106, 174
zoom, 112

www.ingramcontent.com/pod-product-compliance
Lightning Source LLC
Chambersburg PA
CBHW041138110526
44590CB00027B/4054